National 5

Physics

Practice Papers for SQA Exams

Paul Van der Boon

Contents

The instructions and answer grid for completion of Section 1 in each practice paper can be downloaded from www.hoddereducation.co.uk/updatesandextras

HODDER GIBSON
AN HACHETTE UK COMPANY

The Publishers would like to thank the following for permission to reproduce copyright material:

Exam rubrics at the start of Section 1 and Section 2 of each practice paper; Data sheet at the start of each practice paper; CAS on pages v-x; Relationships sheet on pages xi-xiv, reproduced by kind permission of SQA, Copyright © Scottish Qualifications Authority.

Photo credits: p.11 © Shcherbakov Ilya/Shutterstock; p.17 © seksan kingwatcharapong/Shutterstock; p.22 (left) © Kim Steele/Photodisc/Getty Images/ Science, Technology & Medicine 2 54, (right) © StockTrek/Photodisc/Getty Images/ Science, Technology & Medicine 2 54; p.23 © arsgera/123RF.com; p.25 © Nick Rowe/Photodisc/Getty Images / Professional Science 72; p.27 © eugenesergeev/Fotolia; p.29 ©aureliano1704/123RF.com; p.33 © Celso Diniz/123RF.com; p.40 © Ski-erx/Fotolia; p.47 © Celso Diniz/123RF.com; p.54 © marchcattle/123RF.com; p 63 © marcel/Fotolia; p.66 © Kris Christiaens/123RF.com; p.71 (left) © Brian Jackson/Fotolia, (right) © Lars Johansson/Fotolia; p.87 © gary718/123RF.com; p.101 © Imagestate Media (John Foxx) / Global Travel Transport Vol 29; p.103© dell/Fotolia; p.104 © Georgios Kollidas/Fotolia

Orders: please contact Bookpoint Ltd, 130 Park Drive, Milton Park, Abingdon, Oxon OX14 4SE. Telephone: (44) 01235 827720. Fax: (44) 01235 400454. Lines are open 9.00–5.00, Monday to Saturday, with a 24-hour message answering service. Visit our website at www.hoddereducation.co.uk. Hodder Gibson can be contacted direct on: Tel: 0141 333 4650; Fax: 0141 404 8188; email: hoddergibson@hodder.co.uk

First published in 2016 by
Hodder Gibson, an imprint of Hodder Education,
An Hachette UK Company
211 St Vincent Street
Glasgow G2 5QY

Impression number	5 4 3 2 1
Year	2020 2019 2018 2017 2016

Cover photo © artida/123RF.com
Illustrations by Aptara, Inc.
Typeset in DIN Regular, 12/14.4 pts. by Aptara Inc.
Printed in the UK

A catalogue record for this title is available from the British Library

ISBN: 9781471886232

Introduction

National 5 Physics

The three papers included in this book are designed to provide practice and to support revision for the National 5 Physics course assessment question paper (the examination), which is worth 80% of the final grade for this course.

Together, the three papers give overall and comprehensive coverage of the skills, knowledge and understanding needed to pass National 5 Physics.

Design of the papers

Each question paper has been carefully assembled to be similar to a typical National 5 Physics exam paper.

The question paper has a total of 110 marks. The Scottish Qualification Authority (SQA) scale this to 80 marks out of a total of 100 marks, which is 80% of the overall marks for the course assessment.

Each paper is divided into two sections.

Section 1 – The Objective Test contains 20 multiple choice items each worth 1 mark and totalling 20 marks altogether. There is only one correct answer for each question.

Section 2 – Contains restricted and extended-response questions totalling 90 marks altogether. This is scaled to 60 marks by SQA.

For each paper, as far as possible, marks have been distributed proportionally across the three units of the course:

- Electricity and Energy (E&E)
- Waves and Radiation (W&R)
- Dynamics and Space (D&S).

Most of the marks are awarded for applying knowledge and understanding. The remainder of the marks are awarded for applying scientific inquiry, scientific analytical thinking and problem solving skills. These skills are assessed in the question paper in the context of the mandatory knowledge for the course.

Approximately 70% of the marks are set at the standard for the award of Grade C and the remaining 30% are more difficult marks set at the standard for the award of Grade A. Each paper is constructed to represent the typical range of demand in a National 5 Physics paper.

Revision grid

The Revision grid on pages v–x matches every question in the practice papers to the coursework being assessed. The Course Assessment Specification (CAS) identifies the mandatory knowledge and key areas within each unit of the course. Every question is matched to the relevant part in a key area which is being assessed. Each part has been numbered to allow the exact section of a key area to be identified.

The grid includes a section illustrating the type of question where the skills of applying scientific inquiry, scientific analytical thinking and problem solving skills are assessed.

For example, this extract for Paper A:

Key area	Paper A		Paper B		Paper C		Date completed
	Section 1	Section 2	Section 1	Section 2	Section 1	Section 2	
D&S 4.4 Use of an appropriate relationship to solve problems involving weight, mass and gravitational field strength, including on different planets.		9 a)	16	1 b)		11 b) (i)	

indicates that Q9a) in Practice Paper A, Section 2 assesses the key area 'Newton's laws' in the Dynamics and Space unit (part four). For each key area part, you can record your revision progress in the 'Date completed' column.

The question pages have **student margins**, indicating where information can be found in the Hodder Gibson How To Pass National 5 Physics (HTP) book while referencing the relevant area of the Course Assessment Specification (CAS).

Answer section

The answers given on pages 109–144 are the expected answers which follow the National Standard. There may be some questions with more than one acceptable method of reaching the same answer. For example, in 'open-ended' questions, there may be explanations of different physics phenomena which would attract maximum marks. Each answer in this section shows how individual marks are awarded for each part of the question.

Also, in the answers section, there is a 'Hints' column which gives a detailed path of how each answer is obtained, often with guidance on how to order an answer and set out explanations.

Using the practice questions

The N5 Physics exam lasts 2 hours. There are 110 marks available. On average, this would mean 1 mark should take just under a minute. Of course, some questions are more difficult than others, and will take longer to understand and complete. However, too much time spent on one question probably means that some other questions will be rushed.

When using these practice questions to test and improve your knowledge and skills, spend at least as much time answering the questions as you would in the real exam.

Pace your progress through the answers

A question worth 10 marks should take longer than a question worth only 3 marks, for example. Practise as many questions as possible to get used to the style and format of the questions. Use the hints and explanations in the answers section when you get a wrong answer.

When answering questions where a numerical answer has to be calculated, avoid using your calculator to work out an answer and then simply writing the answer without including any working. If you make an error in entering the values into your calculator your answer will be wrong and no marks will be awarded. The answer section illustrates how to set out the different stages of the calculation. Doing this can mean that even if your final answer has been miscalculated, you may still get some marks for showing correct working leading up to your final answer.

Revision grid

Key area	Paper A		Paper B		Paper C		Date completed
	Section 1	Section 2	Section 1	Section 2	Section 1	Section 2	
Unit 1 Energy and Electricity							
E&E 1.1 Knowledge of the principle of 'conservation of energy' applied to examples where energy is transferred between stores. Identification and explanation of 'loss' of energy where energy is transferred.	2			4 b) (iii)		1 c)	
E&E 1.2 Use of an appropriate relationship to solve problems involving potential energy, mass, gravitational field strength and height.	1		1			1 b)	
E&E 1.3 Use of an appropriate relationship to solve problems involving kinetic energy, mass and speed.				10 b) (ii)		1 a)	
E&E 2.2 Use of an appropriate relationship to solve problems involving charge, current and time.	4		2		1		
E&E 2.3 Knowledge of the difference between alternating and direct current.				7 a)			
E&E 3.1 Awareness of the effect of an electric field on a charged particle.	3			1 a)			
E&E 4.1 Use of a V-I graph to determine resistance.					2		
E&E 4.2 Use of an appropriate relationship to solve problems involving potential difference (voltage), current and resistance.		2 a) (i)	3			2 a) (iii)	
E&E 5.2 Knowledge of the circuit symbol, function and application of standard electrical and electronic components including cell, battery, lamp, switch, resistor, variable resistor, voltmeter, ammeter, LED, motor, microphone, loudspeaker, photovoltaic cell, fuse, diode, capacitor, thermistor, LDR, relay, transistor.		2 b) (i)		7 c) (i), (ii)	5	2 a) (i), (ii)	

Key area	Paper A		Paper B		Paper C		Date completed
	Section 1	Section 2	Section 1	Section 2	Section 1	Section 2	
E&E 5.3 For transistors, familiarity with the symbols for an npn transistor and an n-channel enhancement mode MOSFET. Explanation of their function as a switch in transistor switching circuits.						2 b)	
E&E 5.4 Knowledge of current and voltage relationships in series and parallel circuits.	5	1 a)		2 a) 3 a) (i)	4		
E&E 5.5 Use of appropriate relationships to solve problems involving the total resistance of resistors in series and in parallel circuits, and circuits with a combination of series and parallel resistors.		1 c)	4		3		
E&E 6.1 Use of an appropriate relationship to solve problems involving energy, power and time.		3 b)		4 b) (i)		3 b)	
E&E 6.2 Use of appropriate relationships to solve problems involving power, potential difference (voltage), current and resistance in electrical circuits.		1 b)	2	3 a) (ii) 3 b)	6		
E&E 7.4 Use of an appropriate relationship to solve problems involving mass, heat energy, temperature change and specific heat capacity.		3 a)		4 a)		3 a)	
E&E 8.3 Use of an appropriate relationship to carry out calculations involving pressure, force and area.	6			5 b) (ii)		4 b) (i)	
E&E 8.4 Knowledge of the relationship between kelvins and degrees Celsius and the absolute zero of temperature.			6				
E&E 8.5 Explanation of the pressure-volume, pressure-temperature and volume temperature laws qualitatively in terms of a kinetic model.	7	4 b)	5			4 b) (ii)	
E&E 8.6 Use of appropriate relationships to solve problems involving the volume, pressure and kelvin temperature of a fixed mass of gas.		4 a)		5 a)	7	4 a)	

Key area	Paper A		Paper B		Paper C		Date completed
	Section 1	Section 2	Section 1	Section 2	Section 1	Section 2	
Unit 2 Waves and Radiation							
W&R 1.2 Determination of frequency, period, wavelength, amplitude and wave speed for longitudinal and transverse waves.	8			7 b) (i), (ii), (iii)			
W&R 1.3 Use of appropriate relationships to solve problems involving wave speed, frequency, period, wavelength, distance and time.		5 a) 5 b) 7 b) (ii)	7	8 b)		5 a) (i), (ii)	
W&R 1.4 Awareness of the practical limitations of demonstrating diffraction.	9					5 a) (iii)	
W&R 1.5 Comparison of long wave and short wave diffraction.						6 b)	
W&R 2.1 Knowledge of the relative frequency and wavelength of bands of the electromagnetic spectrum with reference to typical sources, detectors and applications.		7 b) (i)		8 a) (i) 8 d)		6 a) (i), (iii)	
W&R 2.2 Knowledge of the qualitative relationship between the frequency and energy associated with a form of radiation.						6 a)(ii)	
W&R 3.1 In ray diagrams showing refraction, identification of the normal, angle of incidence and angle of refraction.		7 a) (ii), (iii)					
W&R 3.2 Description of refraction in terms of change of wave speed, change of wavelength and change of direction (where the angle of incidence is greater than 0°).		7 a) (i)	8 9		8	5 b)	
W&R 4.1 Knowledge of the nature of alpha, beta and gamma radiation, the relative effect of their ionisation, and their relative penetration.	10 11		11	9 c) (iii)	9	8(c)(i)	
W&R 4.2 Use of an appropriate relationship to solve problems involving activity, number of nuclear disintegrations and time.			10		10		
W&R 4.3 Knowledge of background radiation sources.						8 a)	

Key area	Paper A		Paper B		Paper C		Date completed
	Section 1	Section 2	Section 1	Section 2	Section 1	Section 2	
W&R 4.4 Use of appropriate relationships to solve problems involving absorbed dose, equivalent dose, energy, mass and radiation weighting factor.	12	8 b) (i)		9 c)(i), (ii)	11 12		
W&R 4.6 Awareness of equivalent dose rate and exposure safety limits for the public and for workers in radiation industries in terms of annual effective equivalent dose.					13		
W&R 4.7 Use of an appropriate relationship to solve problems involving equivalent dose rate, equivalent dose and time.		8 b) (ii)	12			9 c)	
W&R 4.9 Definition of half-life.		8 a) (i)				8 b) (i)	
W&R 4.10 Use of graphical or numerical data to determine the half-life of a radioactive material.		8 a) (i), (ii) 9 b) (i), (ii)				8 b) (ii) 8 c) (ii)	
W&R 4.11 Qualitative description of fission and fusion, with emphasis on the importance of these processes in the generation of energy.	13	9 a)		9 d)			
Unit 3 Dynamics and Space							
D&S 1.1 Definition of vector and scalar quantities.	14						
D&S 1.2 Identification of force, speed, velocity, distance, displacement, acceleration, mass, time and energy as vector or scalar quantities.					14		
D&S 1.3 Calculation of the resultant of two vector quantities in one dimension or at right angles.		9 b)	13	5 b) (iii) 10 b) (iii)			
D&S 1.4 Determination of displacement and/or distance using scale diagram or calculation.	15						
D&S 1.5 Use of appropriate relationships to solve problems involving velocity, displacement and time		10 b) (ii)		8 c)	15	6 b) (ii)	

Key area	Paper A		Paper B		Paper C		Date completed
	Section 1	Section 2	Section 1	Section 2	Section 1	Section 2	
D&S 2.3 Determination of displacement from a velocity–time graph.		10 b) (i)	14			9 a) (iii)	
D&S 3.2 Determination of acceleration from a velocity–time graph.		10 a) (i)	14		16	9 a) (i)	
D&S 4.1 Applications of Newton's Laws and balanced forces to explain constant velocity, making reference to frictional forces.		10 a) (ii), (iii)		1 c)	17	9 b) 11 a) (iii)	
D&S 4.2 Use of an appropriate relationship to solve problems involving unbalanced force, mass and acceleration for situations where more than one force is acting.	16		15			9 a) (ii) 11 b) (ii)	
D&S 4.3 Use of an appropriate relationship to solve problems involving work done, unbalanced force and distance/displacement.	17			10 a) (ii)		11 a)(i)	
D&S 4.4 Use of an appropriate relationship to solve problems involving weight, mass and gravitational field strength, including on different planets.		9 a)	16	1 b)		11 b) (i)	
D&S 4.5 Knowledge of Newton's second law including its application to space travel, rocket launch and landing.	18		17				
D&S 4.6 Knowledge of Newton's third law and its application to explain motion resulting from a 'reaction' force.	19		18				
D&S 5.1 Explanation of projectile motion.		11 c)	19		18		
D&S 5.2 Use of appropriate relationships to solve problems involving projectile motion from a horizontal launch, including the use of motion graphs.		11 a), b)		10 b) (i)			
D&S 6.3 Qualitative awareness of the relationship between the altitude of a satellite and its period.				8 a) (ii)			

Key area	Paper A		Paper B		Paper C		Date completed
	Section 1	Section 2	Section 1	Section 2	Section 1	Section 2	
D&S 6.6 Awareness of the risks associated with manned space exploration, for example fuel load on takeoff, potential exposure to radiation, pressure differential and challenges of re-entry to a planet's atmosphere.						11 a)(ii)	
D&S 6.7 Use of an appropriate relationship to solve problems involving heat energy, mass and specific latent heat.	20			4 b) (ii)	19		
D&S 7.1 Use of the term 'light year' and conversion between light years and metres.			20			6 a) (iv)	
D&S 7.5 Use of spectral data for known elements, to identify the elements present in stars.					20		
Skills							
Selecting information and presenting information appropriately in a variety of forms.		2 a) (ii)		2 b) (i) 10 a)(i)			
Making predictions based on evidence/ information.		2 b) (ii)		2 b) (ii)			
Drawing valid conclusions and giving explanations supported by evidence/ justification.		3 c) (i)		2 b) (iii)			
Identifying a source of uncertainty and suggesting an improvement to an experiment/practical investigation.		3 c) (ii) 4 c)					
Demonstrating knowledge and understanding of physics by making statements, describing information, providing explanations and integrating knowledge.		6 12				7 10	
Processing information (using calculations and units where appropriate).				5 b) (i)			
Applying knowledge of physics to new situations, interpreting information and solving problems.				6 11			

Relationships sheet

You will be provided with the Relationships sheet in your final exam. Please refer to it as required for each practice paper.

$$E_p = mgh$$

$$E_k = \frac{1}{2}mv^2$$

$$Q = It$$

$$V = IR$$

$$R_T = R_1 + R_2 + \ldots$$

$$\frac{1}{R_T} = \frac{1}{R_1} + \frac{1}{R_2} + \ldots$$

$$V_2 = \left(\frac{R_2}{R_1 + R_2}\right)V_s$$

$$\frac{V_1}{V_2} = \frac{R_1}{R_2}$$

$$P = \frac{E}{t}$$

$$P = IV$$

$$P = I^2R$$

$$P = \frac{V^2}{R}$$

$$E_h = cm\Delta T$$

$$p = \frac{F}{A}$$

$$\frac{pV}{T} = \text{constant}$$

$$p_1V_1 = p_2V_2$$

$$\frac{p_1}{T_1} = \frac{p_2}{T_2}$$

$$\frac{V_1}{T_1} = \frac{V_2}{T_2}$$

$$d = vt$$

$$v = f\lambda$$

$$T = \frac{1}{f}$$

$$A = \frac{N}{t}$$

$$D = \frac{E}{m}$$

$$H = Dw_R$$

$$\dot{H} = \frac{H}{t}$$

$$s = vt$$

$$d = \bar{v}t$$

$$s = \bar{v}t$$

$$a = \frac{v-u}{t}$$

$$W = mg$$

$$F = ma$$

$$E_w = Fd$$

$$E_h = ml$$

Additional relationships

Circle

circumference = $2\pi r$

area = πr^2

Sphere

area = $4\pi r^2$

volume = $\frac{4}{3}\pi r^3$

Trigonometry

$\sin\theta = \frac{\text{opposite}}{\text{hypotenuse}}$

$\cos\theta = \frac{\text{adjacent}}{\text{hypotenuse}}$

$\tan\theta = \frac{\text{opposite}}{\text{adjacent}}$

$\sin^2\theta + \cos^2\theta = 1$

Electron Arrangements of Elements

Key

Atomic number Symbol Electron arrangement Name

Transition Elements

Group 1 (1)	Group 2 (2)	(3)	(4)	(5)	(6)	(7)	(8)	(9)	(10)	(11)	(12)	Group 3 (13)	Group 4 (14)	Group 5 (15)	Group 6 (16)	Group 7 (17)	Group 0 (18)
1 **H** 1 Hydrogen																	2 **He** 2 Helium
3 **Li** 2,1 Lithium	4 **Be** 2,2 Beryllium											5 **B** 2,3 Boron	6 **C** 2,4 Carbon	7 **N** 2,5 Nitrogen	8 **O** 2,6 Oxygen	9 **F** 2,7 Fluorine	10 **Ne** 2,8 Neon
11 **Na** 2,8,1 Sodium	12 **Mg** 2,8,2 Magnesium											13 **Al** 2,8,3 Aluminium	14 **Si** 2,8,4 Silicon	15 **P** 2,8,5 Phosphorus	16 **S** 2,8,6 Sulfur	17 **Cl** 2,8,7 Chlorine	18 **Ar** 2,8,8 Argon
19 **K** 2,8,8,1 Potassium	20 **Ca** 2,8,8,2 Calcium	21 **Sc** 2,8,9,2 Scandium	22 **Ti** 2,8,10,2 Titanium	23 **V** 2,8,11,2 Vanadium	24 **Cr** 2,8,13,1 Chromium	25 **Mn** 2,8,13,2 Manganese	26 **Fe** 2,8,14,2 Iron	27 **Co** 2,8,15,2 Cobalt	28 **Ni** 2,8,16,2 Nickel	29 **Cu** 2,8,18,1 Copper	30 **Zn** 2,8,18,2 Zinc	31 **Ga** 2,8,18,3 Gallium	32 **Ge** 2,8,18,4 Germanium	33 **As** 2,8,18,5 Arsenic	34 **Se** 2,8,18,6 Selenium	35 **Br** 2,8,18,7 Bromine	36 **Kr** 2,8,18,8 Krypton
37 **Rb** 2,8,18,8,1 Rubidium	38 **Sr** 2,8,18,8,2 Strontium	39 **Y** 2,8,18,9,2 Yttrium	40 **Zr** 2,8,18, 10,2 Zirconium	41 **Nb** 2,8,18, 12,1 Niobium	42 **Mo** 2,8,18,13, 1 Molybdenum	43 **Tc** 2,8,18,13, 2 Technetium	44 **Ru** 2,8,18,15, 1 Ruthenium	45 **Rh** 2,8,18,16, 1 Rhodium	46 **Pd** 2,8,18, 18,0 Palladium	47 **Ag** 2,8,18, 18,1 Silver	48 **Cd** 2,8,18, 18,2 Cadmium	49 **In** 2,8,18, 18,3 Indium	50 **Sn** 2,8,18, 18,4 Tin	51 **Sb** 2,8,18, 18,5 Antimony	52 **Te** 2,8,18, 18,6 Tellurium	53 **I** 2,8,18, 18,7 Iodine	54 **Xe** 2,8,18, 18,8 Xenon
55 **Cs** 2,8,18,18, 8,1 Caesium	56 **Ba** 2,8,18,18, 8,2 Barium	57 **La** 2,8,18,18, 9,2 Lanthanum	72 **Hf** 2,8,18,32, 10,2 Hafnium	73 **Ta** 2,8,18, 32,11,2 Tantalum	74 **W** 2,8,18,32, 12,2 Tungsten	75 **Re** 2,8,18,32, 13,2 Rhenium	76 **Os** 2,8,18,32, 14,2 Osmium	77 **Ir** 2,8,18,32, 15,2 Iridium	78 **Pt** 2,8,18,32, 17,1 Platinum	79 **Au** 2,8,18, 32,18,1 Gold	80 **Hg** 2,8,18, 32,18,2 Mercury	81 **Tl** 2,8,18, 32,18,3 Thallium	82 **Pb** 2,8,18, 32,18,4 Lead	83 **Bi** 2,8,18, 32,18,5 Bismuth	84 **Po** 2,8,18, 32,18,6 Polonium	85 **At** 2,8,18, 32,18,7 Astatine	86 **Rn** 2,8,18, 32,18,8 Radon
87 **Fr** 2,8,18,32, 18,8,1 Francium	88 **Ra** 2,8,18,32, 18,8,2 Radium	89 **Ac** 2,8,18,32, 18,9,2 Actinium	104 **Rf** 2,8,18,32, 32,10,2 Rutherfordium	105 **Db** 2,8,18,32, 32,11,2 Dubnium	106 **Sg** 2,8,18,32, 32,12,2 Seaborgium	107 **Bh** 2,8,18,32, 32,13,2 Bohrium	108 **Hs** 2,8,18,32, 32,14,2 Hassium	109 **Mt** 2,8,18,32, 32,15,2 Meitnerium	110 **Ds** 2,8,18,32, 32,17,1 Darmstadtium	111 **Rg** 2,8,18,32, 32,18,1 Roentgenium	112 **Cn** 2,8,18,32, 32,18,2 Copernicium						

Lanthanides	57 **La** 2,8,18, 18,9,2 Lanthanum	58 **Ce** 2,8,18, 20,8,2 Cerium	59 **Pr** 2,8,18,21, 8,2 Praseodymium	60 **Nd** 2,8,18,22, 8,2 Neodymium	61 **Pm** 2,8,18,23, 8,2 Promethium	62 **Sm** 2,8,18,24, 8,2 Samarium	63 **Eu** 2,8,18,25, 8,2 Europium	64 **Gd** 2,8,18,25, 9,2 Gadolinium	65 **Tb** 2,8,18,27, 8,2 Terbium	66 **Dy** 2,8,18,28, 8,2 Dysprosium	67 **Ho** 2,8,18,29, 8,2 Holmium	68 **Er** 2,8,18,30, 8,2 Erbium	69 **Tm** 2,8,18,31, 8,2 Thulium	70 **Yb** 2,8,18,32, 8,2 Ytterbium	71 **Lu** 2,8,18,32, 9,2 Lutetium
Actinides	89 **Ac** 2,8,18,32, 18,9,2 Actinium	90 **Th** 2,8,18,32, 18,10,2 Thorium	91 **Pa** 2,8,18,32, 20,9,2 Protactinium	92 **U** 2,8,18,32, 21,9,2 Uranium	93 **Np** 2,8,18,32, 22,9,2 Neptunium	94 **Pu** 2,8,18,32, 24,8,2 Plutonium	95 **Am** 2,8,18,32, 25,8,2 Americium	96 **Cm** 2,8,18,32, 25,9,2 Curium	97 **Bk** 2,8,18,32, 27,8,2 Berkelium	98 **Cf** 2,8,18,32, 28,8,2 Californium	99 **Es** 2,8,18,32, 29,8,2 Einsteinium	100 **Fm** 2,8,18,32, 30,8,2 Fermium	101 **Md** 2,8,18,32, 31,8,2 Mendelevium	102 **No** 2,8,18,32, 32,8,2 Nobelium	103 **Lr** 2,8,18,32, 32,9,2 Lawrencium

Practice Paper A

National 5 Physics

HODDER GIBSON
LEARN MORE

Data sheet

Speed of light in materials

Material	*Speed* in m s^{-1}
Air	$3{\cdot}0 \times 10^8$
Carbon dioxide	$3{\cdot}0 \times 10^8$
Diamond	$1{\cdot}2 \times 10^8$
Glass	$2{\cdot}0 \times 10^8$
Glycerol	$2{\cdot}1 \times 10^8$
Water	$2{\cdot}3 \times 10^8$

Gravitational field strengths

	Gravitational field strength on the surface in N kg^{-1}
Earth	9·8
Jupiter	23
Mars	3·7
Mercury	3·7
Moon	1·6
Neptune	11
Saturn	9·0
Sun	270
Uranus	8·7
Venus	8·9

Specific latent heat of fusion of materials

Material	*Specific latent heat of fusion* in J kg^{-1}
Alcohol	$0{\cdot}99 \times 10^5$
Aluminium	$3{\cdot}95 \times 10^5$
Carbon dioxide	$1{\cdot}80 \times 10^5$
Copper	$2{\cdot}05 \times 10^5$
Iron	$2{\cdot}67 \times 10^5$
Lead	$0{\cdot}25 \times 10^5$
Water	$3{\cdot}34 \times 10^5$

Specific latent heat of vaporisation of materials

Material	*Specific latent heat of vaporisation* in J kg^{-1}
Alcohol	$11{\cdot}2 \times 10^5$
Carbon dioxide	$3{\cdot}77 \times 10^5$
Glycerol	$8{\cdot}30 \times 10^5$
Turpentine	$2{\cdot}90 \times 10^5$
Water	$22{\cdot}6 \times 10^5$

Speed of sound in materials

Material	*Speed* in m s^{-1}
Aluminium	5200
Air	340
Bone	4100
Carbon dioxide	270
Glycerol	1900
Muscle	1600
Steel	5200
Tissue	1500
Water	1500

Specific heat capacity of materials

Material	*Specific heat capacity* in J kg^{-1} °C^{-1}
Alcohol	2350
Aluminium	902
Copper	386
Glass	500
Ice	2100
Iron	480
Lead	128
Oil	2130
Water	4180

Melting and boiling points of materials

Material	*Melting point* in °C	*Boiling point* in °C
Alcohol	−98	65
Aluminium	660	2470
Copper	1077	2567
Glycerol	18	290
Lead	328	1737
Iron	1537	2737

Radiation weighting factors

Type of radiation	*Radiation weighting factor*
alpha	20
beta	1
fast neutrons	10
gamma	1
slow neutrons	3
X-rays	1

SECTION 1

SECTION 1— 20 MARKS

Attempt ALL questions – instructions/answer grid available at www.hoddereducation.co.uk/updatesandextras

Reference may be made to the Data sheet on Page 2 and to the Relationships sheet.

STUDENT MARGIN

1 A ball is dropped vertically from a height of 1·20 m to the ground and rebounds as shown.

The mass of the ball is 0·40 kg.

After the rebound the ball reaches a height 0·25 m lower than the release height.

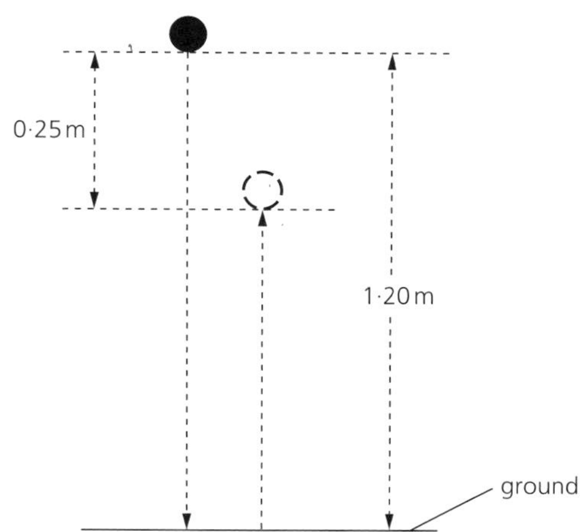

The amount of energy lost is

A 0·10 J
B 0·15 J
C 0·98 J
D 3·7 J
E 4·7 J.

CAS
E&E 1.2
HTP
Page 9

2 The total mass of a go-cart and driver is 200 kg. While braking, the cart and driver are brought to rest from a speed of 10 m s^{-1} in a time of 8·0 s.

The maximum energy which could be transformed into heat in the brakes is

A 2000 J
B 10 000 J
C 16 000 J
D 20 000 J
E 40 000 J.

CAS
E&E 1.1
HTP
Page 9

3 Atomic particles electrons, protons and neutrons are directed into an electric field as shown in the diagram.

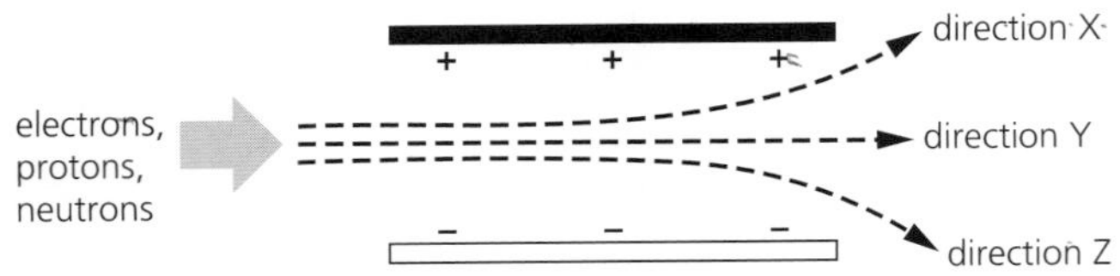

Which row in the table correctly identifies how the particles are deflected?

	Direction X	*Direction Y*	*Direction Z*
A	electrons	protons	neutrons
B	protons	electrons	neutrons
C	neutrons	electrons	protons
D	neutrons	protons	electrons
E	electrons	neutrons	protons

4 The current in a 16 Ω resistor is 4 A.

The charge passing through the resistor in 8 seconds is

A 2 C
B 4 C
C 8 C
D 32 C
E 128 C.

5 Resistors are connected in the following circuit as shown.

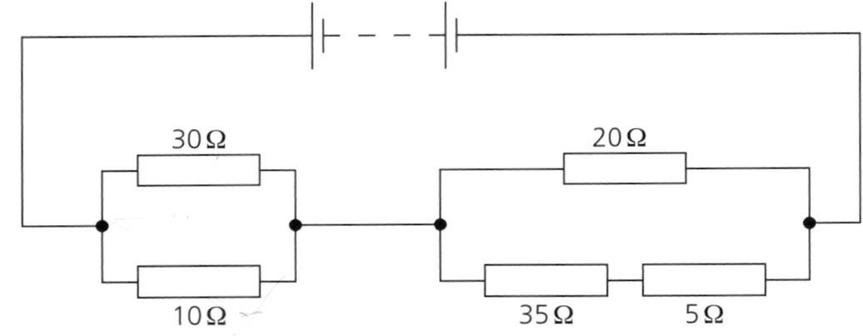

In which resistor is the current **greatest**?

A 5 Ω
B 10 Ω
C 20 Ω
D 30 Ω
E 35 Ω

STUDENT MARGIN

CAS E&E 3.1 HTP Page 11

CAS E&E 2.2 HTP Page 12

CAS E&E 5.4 HTP Page 18

6 The outside pressure on a submarine beneath the sea is $3{\cdot}0 \times 10^{6}$ Pa. The air pressure inside the submarine is $1{\cdot}0 \times 10^{5}$ Pa.

The area of a door hatch on the submarine is $1{\cdot}8\,m^2$.

What is the inward force on the door hatch due to the pressure difference?

A $1{\cdot}61 \times 10^{6}$ N
B $1{\cdot}72 \times 10^{6}$ N
C $5{\cdot}22 \times 10^{6}$ N
D $5{\cdot}40 \times 10^{6}$ N
E $5{\cdot}58 \times 10^{6}$ N

7 A student investigates the relationship between the pressure and kelvin temperature of a fixed mass of gas at constant volume.

Which graph correctly shows this relationship?

A

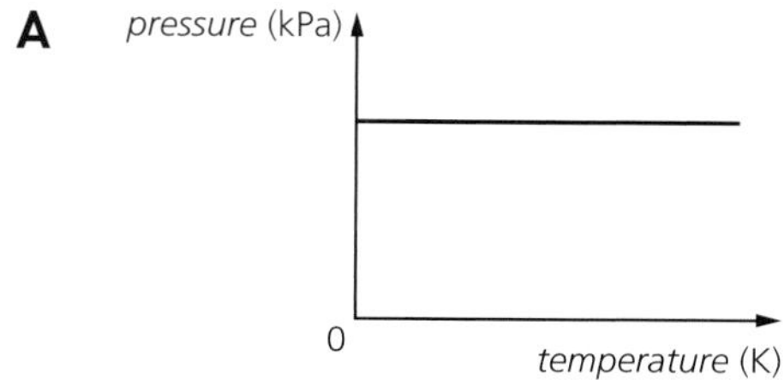

B

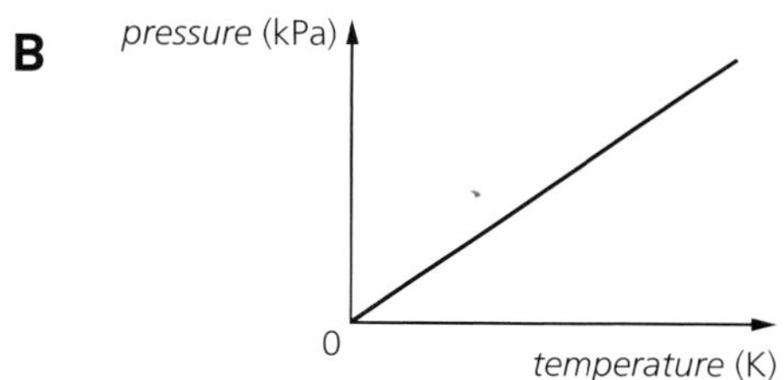

C

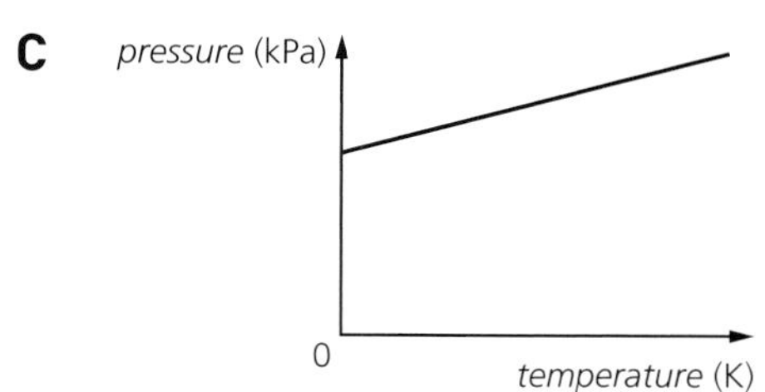

D

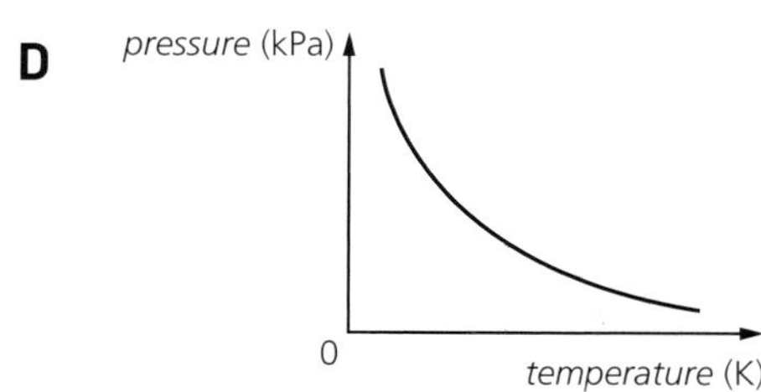

E

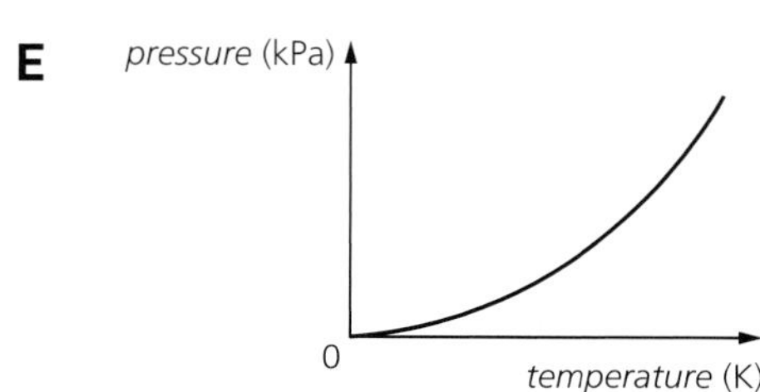

STUDENT MARGIN

CAS
E&E 8.3
HTP
Page 51

CAS
E&E 8.5
HTP
Page 55

8 The diagram gives information about a wave.

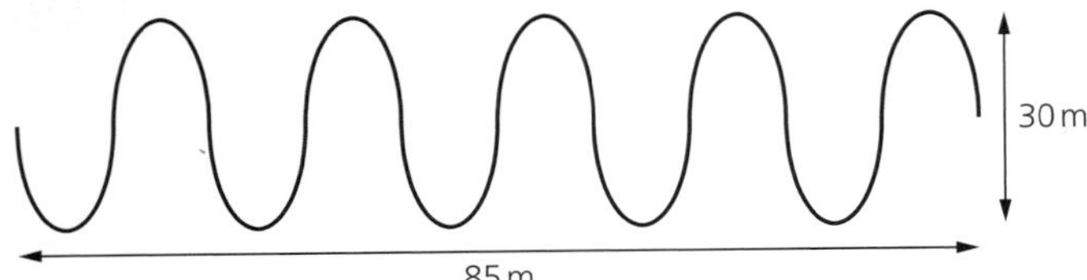

The time taken for the wave to travel 85 m is 2·5 s.

The following statements are made about the wave.

I The speed of the wave is 34 m s^{-1}.
II The frequency of the wave is 2 Hz.
III The amplitude of the wave is 30 m.

Which of these statements is/are correct?

A I only
B II only
C I and II only
D I and III only
E I, II and III

STUDENT MARGIN

CAS
W&R1.2
HTP
Page 58

9 Water waves are produced in a ripple tank. The waves reach a barrier and are diffracted.

Which diagram correctly shows the diffraction in the ripple tank?

A

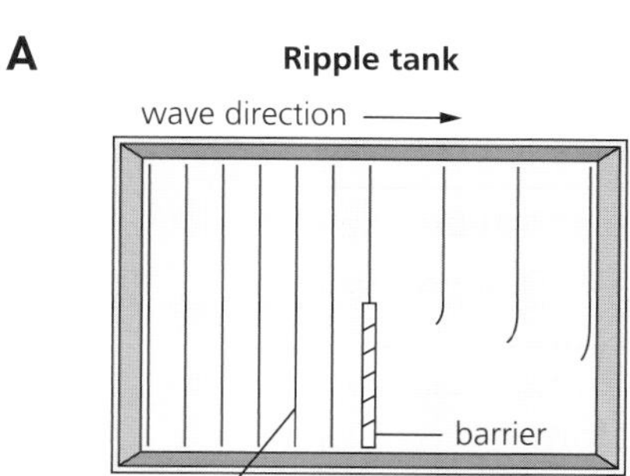

B

Ripple tank
wave direction
barrier
wave crest

C

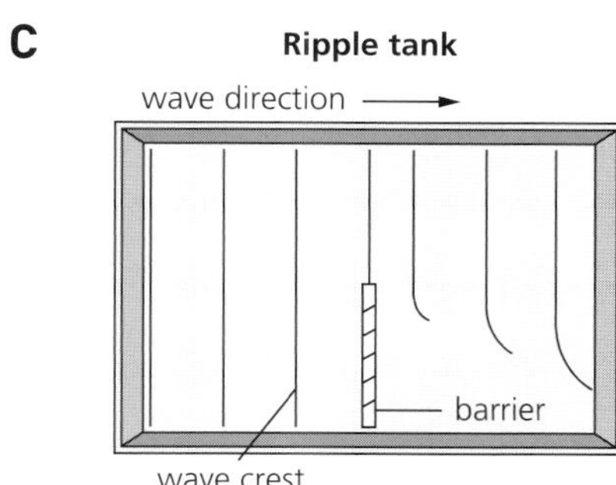

D

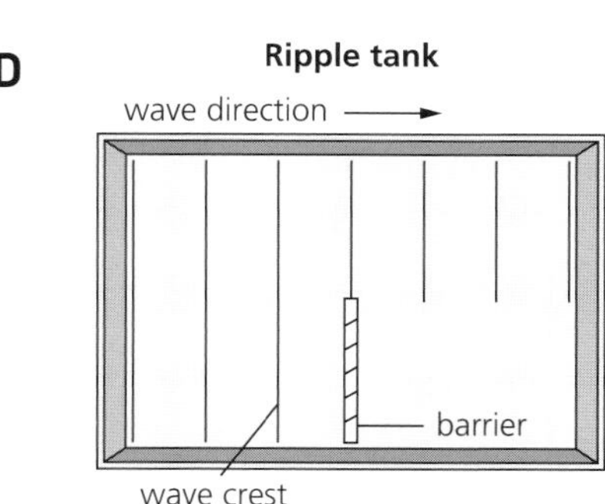

E

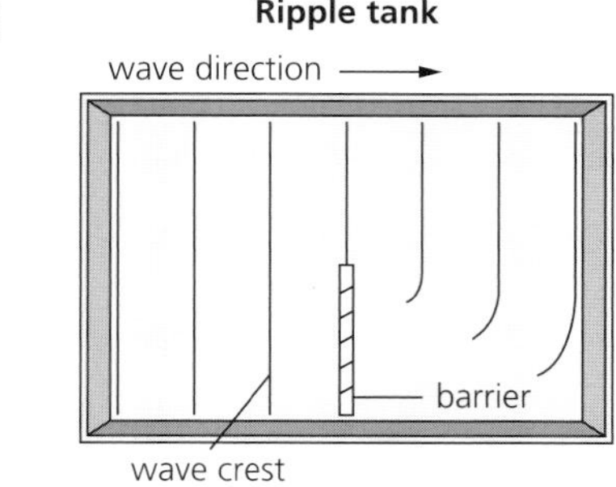

STUDENT MARGIN

CAS W&R1.4 HTP Page 60

10 Which row in the table correctly describes alpha (α) and beta (β) radiations?

	α	β
A	helium nucleus emitted during the radioactive decay of an atom	electron emitted during the radioactive decay of an atom
B	helium nucleus emitted during the radioactive decay of an atom	electromagnetic radiation emitted during the radioactive decay of an atom
C	electromagnetic radiation emitted during radioactive decay of an atom	electron emitted during the radioactive decay of an atom
D	electron emitted during the radioactive decay of an atom	helium nucleus emitted during the radioactive decay of an atom
E	electromagnetic radiation emitted during radioactive decay of an atom	helium nucleus emitted during the radioactive decay of an atom

STUDENT MARGIN

CAS W&R4.1 HTP Page 69

11 A ratemeter was used to measure the background count rate in a laboratory.

The background count rate was measured at 4 counts per second.

The ratemeter was then used to take measurements of the count rate from a radioactive source.

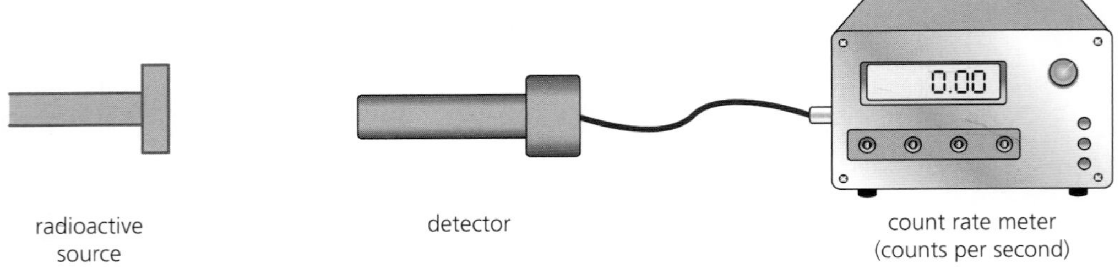

Absorbing materials were placed in turn between the source and detector and the results given in the table.

Absorbing material	*Count rate (counts per second)*
No material	75
Sheet of paper	75
3 mm of aluminium	40
10 mm of lead	8

The radiation emitted by the source is

A α only

B γ only

C α and β only

D β and γ only

E α, β and γ.

CAS W&R4.1 HTP Page 69

12 A tissue sample has a mass of 0·08 kg. The tissue receives an absorbed dose of 24 μGy from alpha particles in 3 minutes.

The energy absorbed by the tissue is

A 1·92 μJ
B 5·76 μJ
C 24·0 μJ
D 300 μJ
E 3000 μJ.

STUDENT MARGIN

CAS W&R4.4 HTP Page 70

13 The following statements refer to nuclear fission and fusion.

I During nuclear fusion a large nucleus splits into smaller nuclei.
II During nuclear fission neutrons are emitted.
III During nuclear fission and nuclear fusion energy is released.

Which of the statements is/are correct?

A I only
B II only
C III only
D I and II only
E II and III only

CAS W&R4.11 HTP Page 75, 76

14 Which of the following contains one vector and one scalar quantity?

A Time, energy
B Force, mass
C Acceleration, displacement
D Speed, time
E Velocity, force

CAS D&S1.1 HTP Page 78

STUDENT MARGIN

15 A cyclist follows the route shown in the diagram.

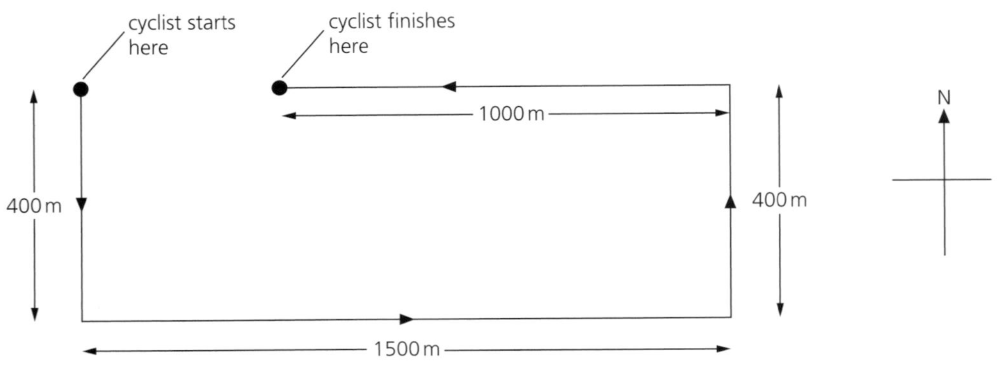

Which row in the table shows the total distance cycled and the final displacement of the cyclist from start to finish?

	Total distance	*Final displacement*
A	3300 m	500 m East
B	3300 m	1000 m East
C	3800 m	1000 m West
D	3800 m	500 m East
E	3300 m	1000 m West

CAS D&S1.4 HTP Page 78

16 A constant force of 54 N pulls a wooden block of mass 5 kg on a track. The block is moving in the direction shown.

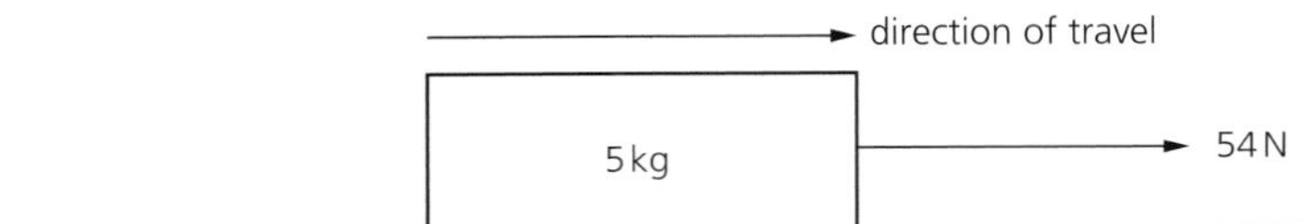

At one instant, the block is **decelerating** at 1·2 ms^{-2}.

The force of friction acting on the block at this instant is

A zero
B 48 N
C 54 N
D 60 N
E 114 N.

CAS D&S4.2 HTP Page 95

17 A builder pushes a wheelbarrow of total mass 50 kg along a path with a force of 20 N at a constant speed of $4{\cdot}0\ m\ s^{-1}$ for a distance of 120 m.

The force of friction acting on the wheelbarrow is 20 N.

The work done on the wheelbarrow by the builder is

A 0 J
B 400 J
C 490 J
D 2400 J
E 9600 J.

STUDENT MARGIN

CAS D&S4.3 HTP Page 100

18 At launch, an Apollo lunar ascent module accelerated vertically upward from the surface of the Moon at $1{\cdot}4\ m\ s^{-2}$. The mass of the module was 5000 kg.

What was the size of the upward thrust acting on the ascent module at this time?

A 7000 N
B 8000 N
C 15 000 N
D 49 000 N
E 56 000 N

CAS D&S4.5 HTP Page 94

19 An aircraft engine exerts a force on the air.

Which of the following completes the 'Newton pair' of forces?

A The force of friction exerts a force between the air and the engine
B The Earth exerts a force on the engine
C The force of friction exerts a force between the engine and the air
D The engine exerts a force on the Earth
E The air exerts a force on the engine

STUDENT MARGIN

CAS
D&S4.6
HTP
Page 95

20 A sample of water is at a temperature of 0 °C.

$9{\cdot}29 \times 10^5$ J of heat energy is removed from the sample.

The mass of water changed into ice is

A 0·36 kg
B 0·41 kg
C 2·43 kg
D 2·78 kg
E $3{\cdot}11 \times 10^{11}$ kg.

CAS
D&S6.7
HTP
Page 110

[END OF SECTION 1]

SECTION 2

SECTION 2 — 90 MARKS

Attempt ALL questions.

Reference may be made to the Data sheet on Page 2 of the question paper and to the Relationships sheet.

Care should be taken to give an appropriate number of significant figures in the final answers to calculations.

Write your answers clearly in the spaces provided in this paper. Any rough work must be written in this paper. You should score through your rough work when you have written your final copy.

Use **blue** or **black** ink.

MARKS | STUDENT MARGIN

1 The brightness of three identical lamps is controlled in the circuit shown.

The variable resistor is adjusted until the lamps operate at their correct voltage of 4·5 V.

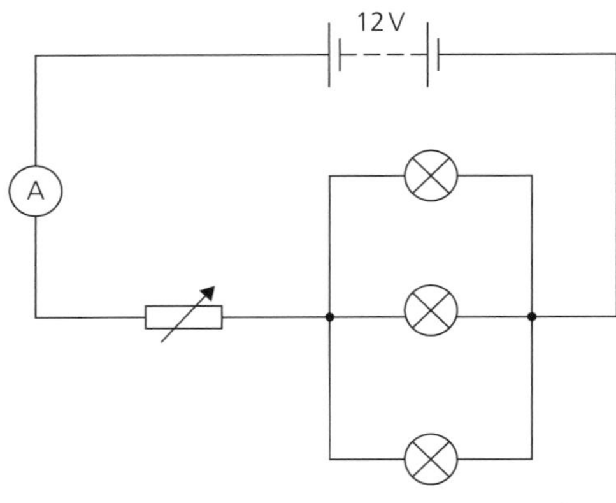

a) The reading on the ammeter is 1·5 A when the lamps operate at their correct voltage.

Calculate the current in one lamp. **1**

Space for working and answer

CAS E&E5.4 HTP Page 19

b) Calculate the power developed in one lamp when operating at its correct voltage. **3**

Space for working and answer

CAS E&E6.2 HTP Page 26

c) An identical lamp is added in parallel with the three lamps.

What happens to the reading on the ammeter? **2**

You must explain your answer.

CAS E&E5.5 HTP Page 22

MARKS STUDENT MARGIN

2 An LDR is used as a light sensor in a circuit to monitor the light level outside a greenhouse. When the light level outside the greenhouse falls below a certain level, lamps are switched on inside the greenhouse. Part of the circuit is shown.

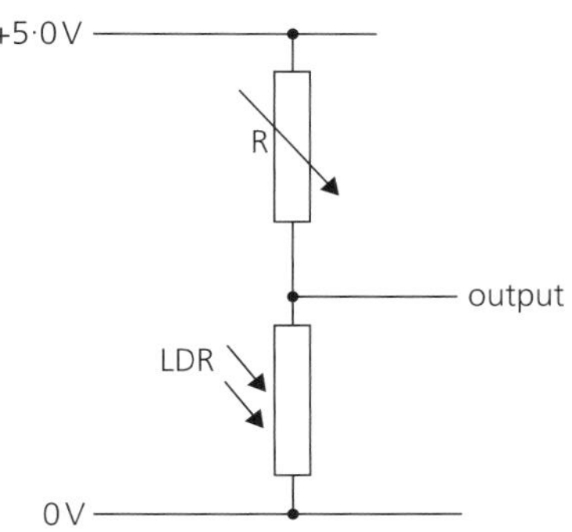

a) **(i)** The variable resistor R is set at a resistance of 2250 Ω.

Calculate the resistance of the LDR when the voltage across the LDR is 2·0 V. **4**

Space for working and answer

CAS E&E4.2 HTP Page 43

The graph shows how the resistance of the LDR varies with the outside light level.

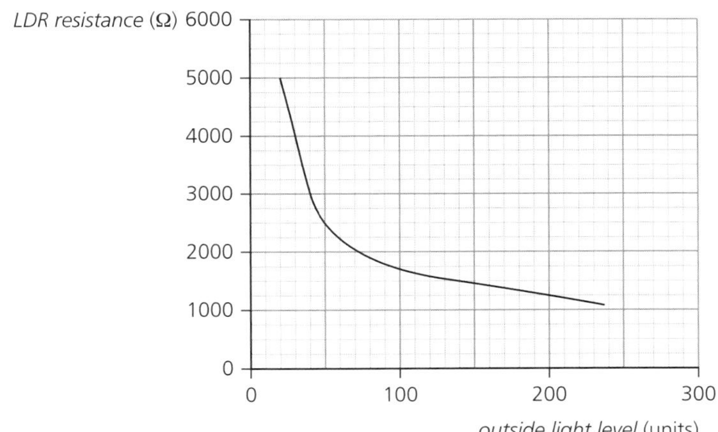

(ii) Use the graph to determine the outside light level when the voltage across the LDR is 2·0 V. **1**

CAS Skill

MARKS | STUDENT MARGIN

2 (continued)

b) The circuit is now connected to a switching circuit to operate the lamps inside the greenhouse.

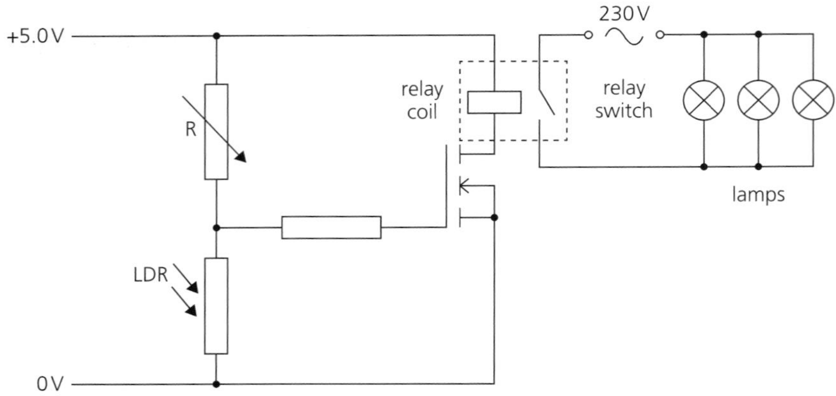

(i) Explain how the circuit operates to switch on the lamps when the outside light level falls below a certain value. **3**

CAS
E&E5.2
HTP
Page46

(ii) The resistance of the variable resistor R is now increased. **3**

What effect does this have on the outside light level at which the lamps will switch on?

You must justify your answer.

CAS
Skill

MARKS STUDENT MARGIN

3 A deep fat fryer is used in a kitchen to fry vegetables.

The rating plate of the deep fat fryer is shown.

frequency	50 Hz
voltage	230 V
power	1500 W

a) The deep fat fryer contains 2·8 kg of vegetable oil at an initial temperature of 20 °C. The specific heat capacity of the oil is 1800 J kg^{-1} °C^{-1}.

Calculate the energy required to raise the temperature of the oil to 170 °C. **3**

Space for working and answer

CAS E&E7.4 HTP Page 49

b) Calculate the minimum time required to heat the oil to 170 °C. **3**

Space for working and answer

CAS E&E6.1 HTP Page 26

3 (continued)

c) In practice it requires more time than calculated to heat the oil.

(i) Explain why more time is required. **1**

CAS Skill

(ii) Suggest one way of reducing this additional time. **1**

CAS Skill

MARKS STUDENT MARGIN

4 A student investigates the relationship between the pressure and temperature of a fixed mass of gas at constant volume. A diagram of the apparatus used for the investigation is shown.

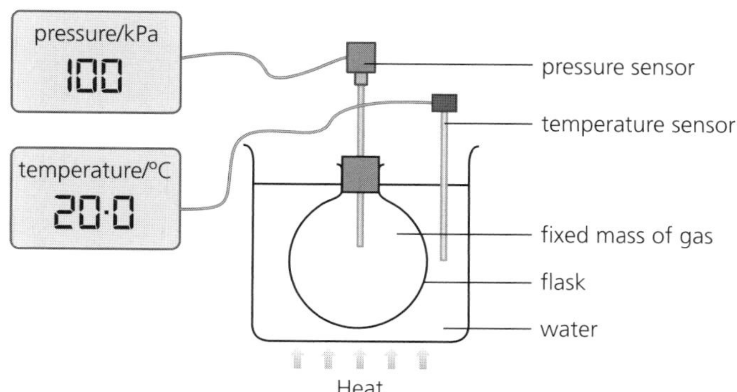

The gas temperature and pressure are obtained using sensors connected to displays.

The gas is slowly heated and the displayed results are recorded in a table.

The volume of the gas remains constant during the investigation.

Some of the results are shown.

Pressure (kPa)	100			
Temperature (°C)	20·0	28·0		

a) Calculate the pressure of the gas when the temperature is 28·0 °C. **3**

Space for working and answer

CAS E&E8.6 HTP Page 55

4 (continued)

	MARKS	STUDENT MARGIN
b) Use the kinetic model to explain the change in gas pressure as the temperature increases.	3	CAS E&E8.5 HTP Page 55
c) Suggest a change which can be made to the apparatus to improve the experiment.	1	CAS Skill

MARKS STUDENT MARGIN

5 A news reporter in a remote area communicates with the news head office by using a satellite phone that uses microwaves.

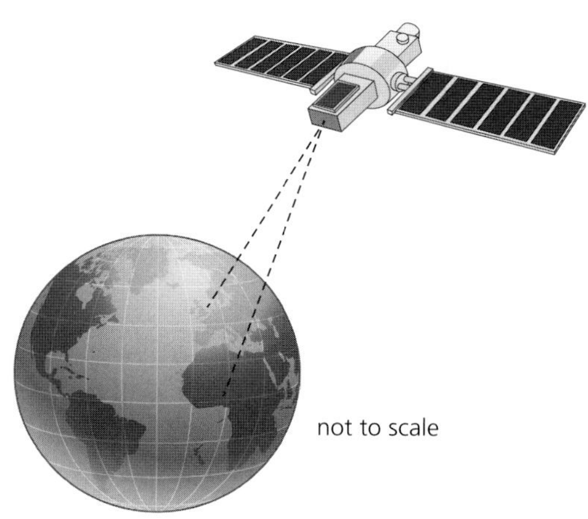

The period of the microwaves is $4{\cdot}0 \times 10^{-10}$ s.

a) Calculate the frequency of the microwaves. **3**

Space for working and answer

CAS W&R1.3 HTP Page 59

b) Calculate the wavelength of the microwaves. **3**

Space for working and answer

CAS W&R1.3 HTP Page 60

MARKS STUDENT MARGIN

6 When carrying out research into astronomical objects, scientists use information obtained from different parts of the electromagnetic spectrum, which is detected in space.

Use your knowledge of physics to comment on the use of different parts of the electromagnetic spectrum in obtaining information about astronomical objects. 3

CAS

Skill

MARKS STUDENT MARGIN

7 a) (i) Refraction of light occurs in spectacle glass lenses.

Explain what is meant by the term refraction. **1**

CAS W&R3.2 HTP Page 65

The diagram shows a light ray entering a glass block.

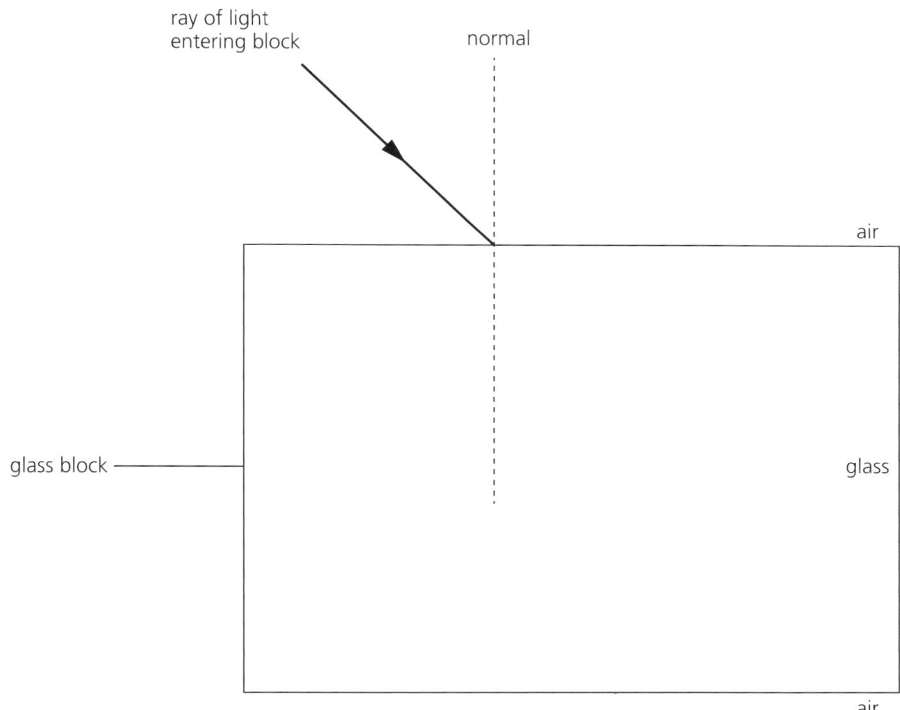

CAS W&R3.1 HTP Page 65

(ii) Complete the diagram to show the path of the light ray inside the block and after it emerges from the block. **2**

(iii) Indicate an angle of incidence, *i*, on the diagram. **1**

CAS W&R3.1 HTP Page 65

MARKS STUDENT MARGIN

7 (continued)

b) The electromagnetic spectrum is shown in order of increasing values of frequency.

Television and radio waves	Microwaves	P	Visible light	Q	X rays	Gamma rays

Increasing frequency →

(i) Identify radiations P and Q. **2**

CAS W&R2.1 HTP Page 62

(ii) Radio waves are sent from Earth to Jupiter. Jupiter is $6{\cdot}7 \times 10^{11}$ m from Earth.

Calculate the time taken for radio waves from Earth to reach Jupiter. **3**

Space for working and answer

CAS W&R1.3 HTP Page 62

MARKS STUDENT MARGIN

8 A university technician is investigating a radioactive material.

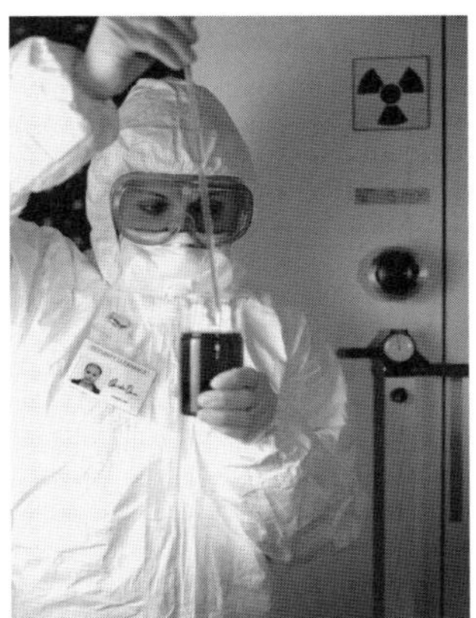

The activity of the material over a period of time is shown in the graph.

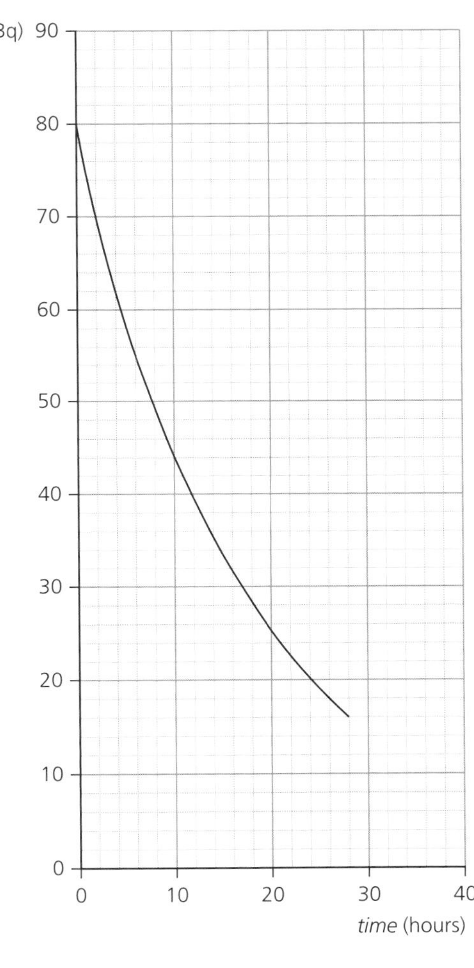

8 (continued)

MARKS | STUDENT MARGIN

a) **(i)** State what is meant by the term *half-life*. **1**

CAS W&R4.9 HTP Page 73

(ii) Use information from the graph to determine the half-life of the radioactive material. **1**

CAS W&R4.10 HTP Page 74

(iii) The initial activity of the material is 80 kBq.

Determine the activity of the material after three half-lives. **2**

Space for working and answer

CAS W&R4.10 HTP Page 74

b) While working with the radioactive material for 3 hours, the technician's hands receive an absorbed dose of 15·0 μGy. The radiation from the material has a radiation weighting factor of 2.

(i) Calculate the equivalent dose received by the technician's hands. **3**

Space for working and answer

CAS W&R4.4 HTP Page 71

(ii) Calculate the equivalent dose rate for the radiation received by the technician's hands. **3**

Space for working and answer

CAS W&R4.7 HTP Page 71

MARKS STUDENT MARGIN

9 A cruise ship is sailing due East at a constant speed on a calm sea.

The cruise ship and its passengers have a total mass of $9 \cdot 7 \times 10^7$ kg.

a) Calculate the total weight of the cruise ship and its passengers. 3

Space for working and answer

CAS D&S4.4 HTP Page 91

9 (continued)

MARKS STUDENT MARGIN

b) While at sea, the cruise ship's engines produce a force of $4{\cdot}6 \times 10^3$ N due East. The cruise ship encounters a strong tide from North to South, which exerts a force of $1{\cdot}8 \times 10^3$ N.

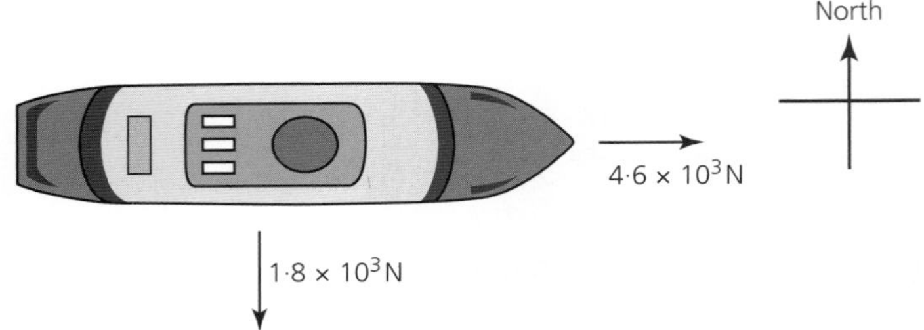

By scale drawing, or otherwise, determine the resultant force acting on the cruise ship. **4**

Space for working and answer

CAS
D&S1.3
HTP
Page 97

MARKS STUDENT MARGIN

10 A cyclist attempts to beat a record time for cycling along a straight, level cycle track. The attempt was recorded by a news camera team on a motor cycle alongside the cyclist.

The graph shows the speed of the cyclist during the attempt.

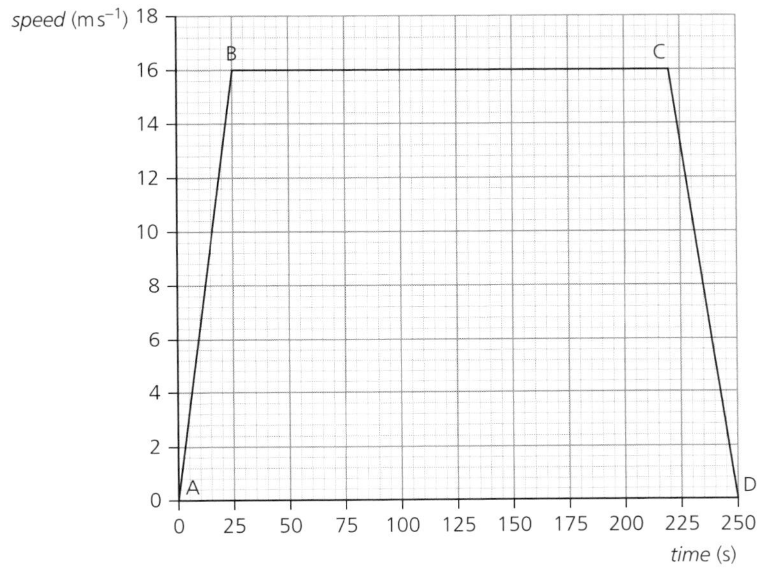

a) **(i)** Calculate the acceleration of the cyclist between C and D. **3**

Space for working and answer

CAS D&S3.2 HTP Page 86

(ii) Describe the motion of the cyclist between B and C. **1**

CAS D&S4.1 HTP Page 85

		MARKS	STUDENT MARGIN
10 a) (continued)			
(iii)	On the drawing of the cyclist, draw and name the horizontal forces acting on the cyclist between B and C.  You **must** indicate the direction of each force.	2	CAS D&S4.1 HTP Page 93
b) (i)	Calculate the total distance travelled by the cyclist. *Space for working and answer*	3	CAS D&S2.3 HTP Page 85
(ii)	Calculate the average speed of the cyclist. *Space for working and answer*	3	CAS D&S1.5 HTP Page 79

National 5 Physics

HODDER GIBSON
LEARN MORE

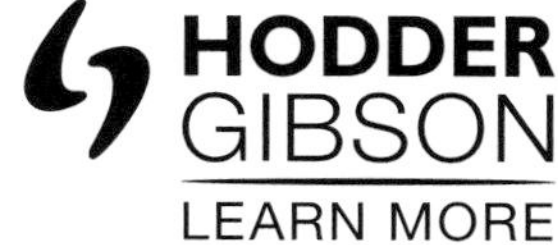

Data sheet

Speed of light in materials

Material	*Speed* in m s^{-1}
Air	$3{\cdot}0 \times 10^8$
Carbon dioxide	$3{\cdot}0 \times 10^8$
Diamond	$1{\cdot}2 \times 10^8$
Glass	$2{\cdot}0 \times 10^8$
Glycerol	$2{\cdot}1 \times 10^8$
Water	$2{\cdot}3 \times 10^8$

Gravitational field strengths

	Gravitational field strength on the surface in N kg^{-1}
Earth	9·8
Jupiter	23
Mars	3·7
Mercury	3·7
Moon	1·6
Neptune	11
Saturn	9·0
Sun	270
Uranus	8·7
Venus	8·9

Specific latent heat of fusion of materials

Material	*Specific latent heat of fusion* in J kg^{-1}
Alcohol	$0{\cdot}99 \times 10^5$
Aluminium	$3{\cdot}95 \times 10^5$
Carbon dioxide	$1{\cdot}80 \times 10^5$
Copper	$2{\cdot}05 \times 10^5$
Iron	$2{\cdot}67 \times 10^5$
Lead	$0{\cdot}25 \times 10^5$
Water	$3{\cdot}34 \times 10^5$

Specific latent heat of vaporisation of materials

Material	*Specific latent heat of vaporisation* in J kg^{-1}
Alcohol	$11{\cdot}2 \times 10^5$
Carbon dioxide	$3{\cdot}77 \times 10^5$
Glycerol	$8{\cdot}30 \times 10^5$
Turpentine	$2{\cdot}90 \times 10^5$
Water	$22{\cdot}6 \times 10^5$

Speed of sound in materials

Material	*Speed* in m s^{-1}
Aluminium	5200
Air	340
Bone	4100
Carbon dioxide	270
Glycerol	1900
Muscle	1600
Steel	5200
Tissue	1500
Water	1500

Specific heat capacity of materials

Material	*Specific heat capacity* in J kg^{-1} °C^{-1}
Alcohol	2350
Aluminium	902
Copper	386
Glass	500
Ice	2100
Iron	480
Lead	128
Oil	2130
Water	4180

Melting and boiling points of materials

Material	*Melting point* in °C	*Boiling point* in °C
Alcohol	−98	65
Aluminium	660	2470
Copper	1077	2567
Glycerol	18	290
Lead	328	1737
Iron	1537	2737

Radiation weighting factors

Type of radiation	*Radiation weighting factor*
alpha	20
beta	1
fast neutrons	10
gamma	1
slow neutrons	3
X-rays	1

SECTION 1

SECTION 1—20 MARKS

Attempt ALL questions – instructions/answer grid available at www.hoddereducation.co.uk/updatesandextras

Reference may be made to the Data sheet on Page 36 and to the Relationships sheet.

STUDENT MARGIN

1 A ball is released from rest and allowed to roll 1·2 m down a straight track as shown.

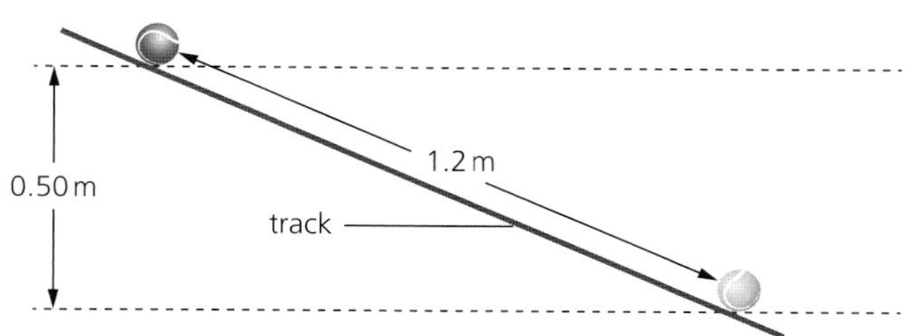

The mass of the ball is 0·40 kg. There is a constant frictional force of 8 N acting on the ball.

The change in the gravitational potential energy of the ball is

A 1·96 J
B 5·88 J
C 10·04 J
D 12·0 J
E 13·96 J.

CAS E&E1.2 HTP Page 9

2 The rating plate of an electric shower heater is shown.

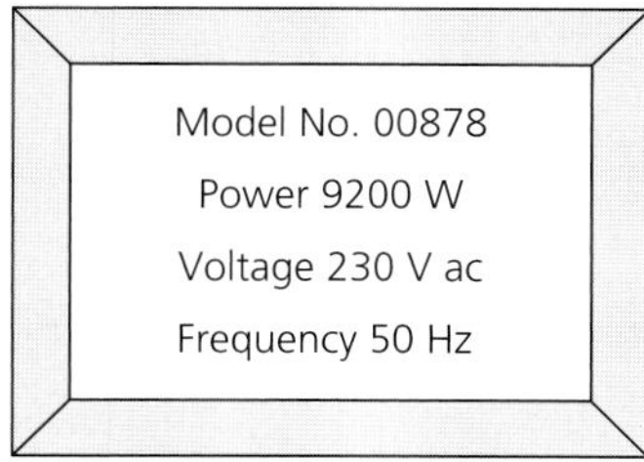

Model No. 00878
Power 9200 W
Voltage 230 V ac
Frequency 50 Hz

The charge that passes through the element of the shower heater in 5 minutes is

A 0·125 C
B 7·5 C
C 200 C
D 12 000 C
E 69 000 C.

CAS E&E2.2, E&E6.2 HTP Page 12,26

3 The circuit shows two resistors connected to a supply of 6 V.

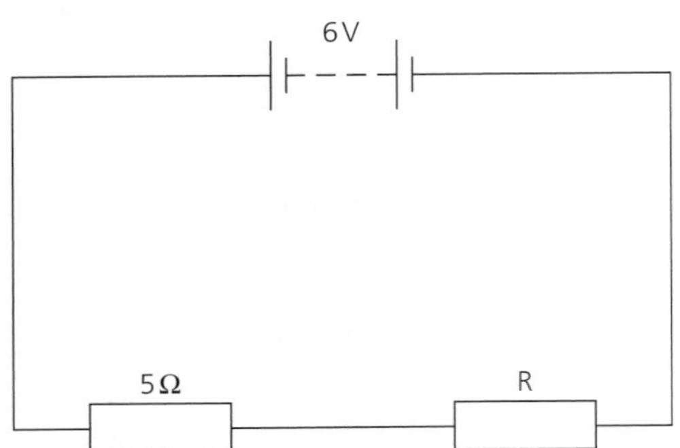

The current in the 5 Ω resistor is 0·5 A.

The resistance of resistor R is

A 5 Ω
B 7 Ω
C 12 Ω
D 17 Ω
E 60 Ω.

4 Four resistors are connected as shown.

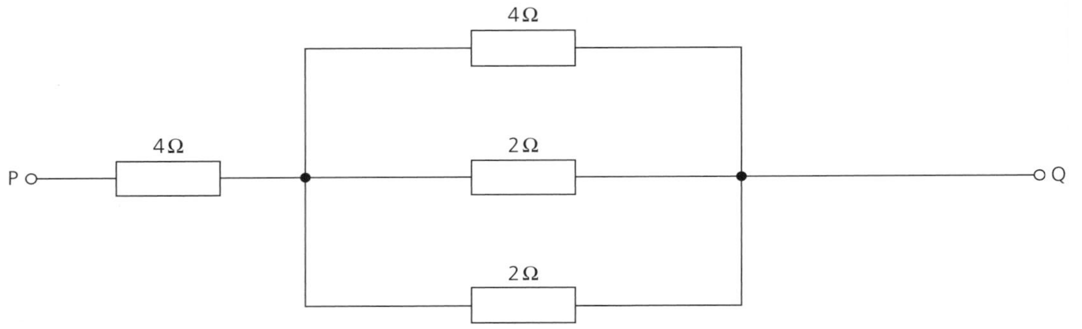

The resistance between P and Q is

A 0·67 Ω
B 3·25 Ω
C 4·8 Ω
D 5·25 Ω
E 7 Ω.

STUDENT MARGIN

CAS E&E4.2 HTP Page 17

CAS E&E5.5 HTP Page 23

STUDENT MARGIN

5 A syringe filled with air is sealed with a stopper.

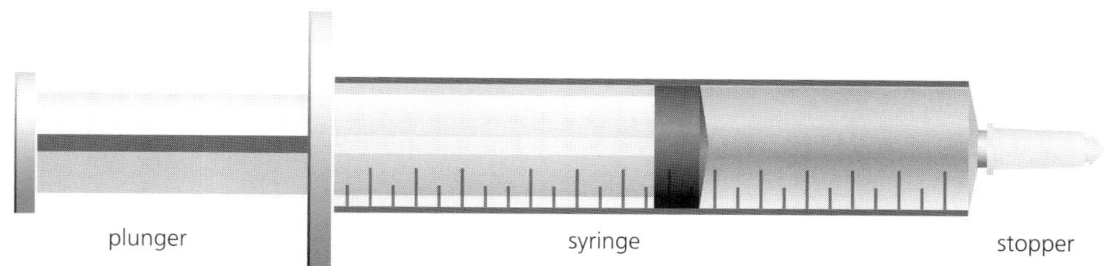

The plunger is slowly pressed into the syringe causing the volume of air to be reduced, and the air pressure to increase. The temperature remains constant during this process.

Which of the following statements is/are correct?

I The air molecules collide with the walls inside the syringe with greater force.

II The air molecules collide with the walls inside the syringe more often.

III The average speed of the air molecules inside the syringe increases.

A I only
B I and II only
C II only
D III only
E I and III only

CAS E&E8.5 HTP Page 53

6 Water at a temperature of 70 °C is cooled until it becomes ice at −15 °C.

The temperature change is

A 55 K
B 85 K
C 328 K
D 358 K
E 631 K.

CAS E&E8.4 HTP Page 57

7 A parakeet can hear sounds of wavelength ranging from 0·04 m to 1·7 m.

If the speed of sound in air is 340 m s^{-1}, the highest frequency the parakeet can hear is

A 13·6 Hz
B 200 Hz
C 578 Hz
D 8·5 kHz
E 85 kHz.

8 For a ray of light travelling from air into glass, which of the following statements is/are correct?

I The speed of light sometimes changes.
II The speed of light always changes.
III The wavelength of light sometimes changes.
IV The wavelength of light always changes.

A I only
B III only
C I and III only
D II and III only
E II and IV only

STUDENT MARGIN

CAS W&R1.3 HTP Page 59

CAS W&R3.2 HTP Page 65

9 A ray of green light emerges from a glass block into air.

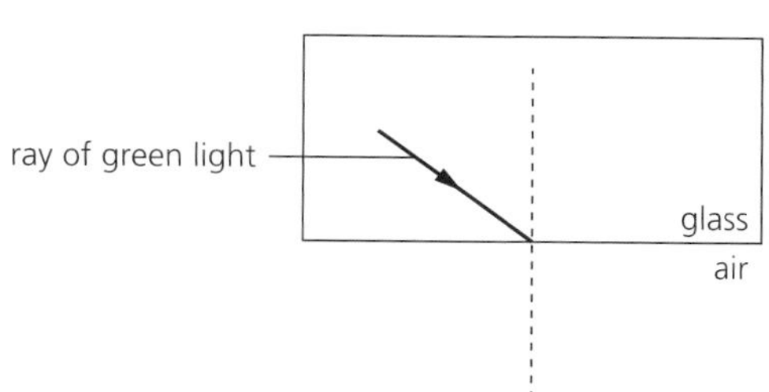

Which diagram correctly represents the ray of light when it emerges from the glass block?

A

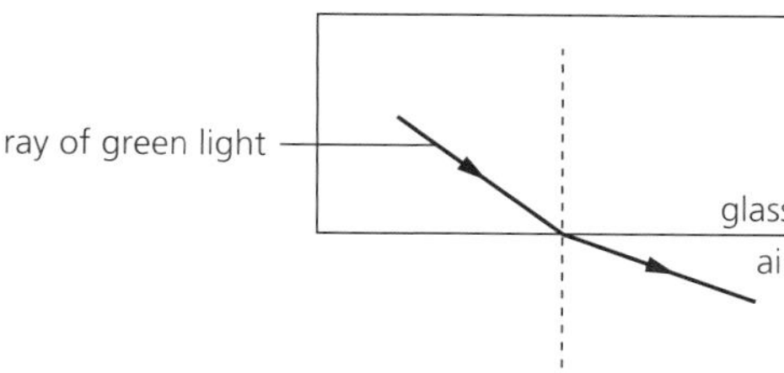

B

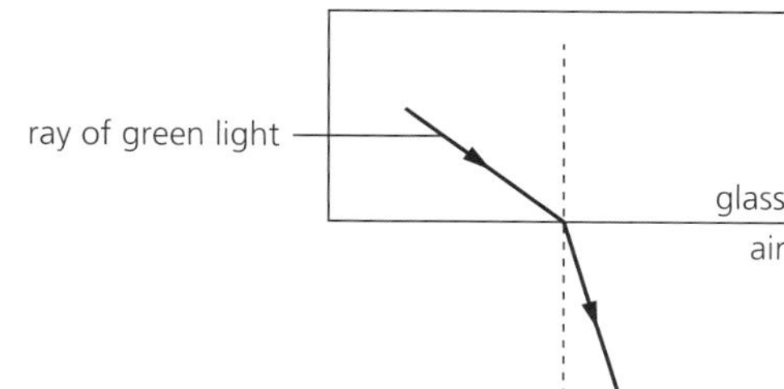

C

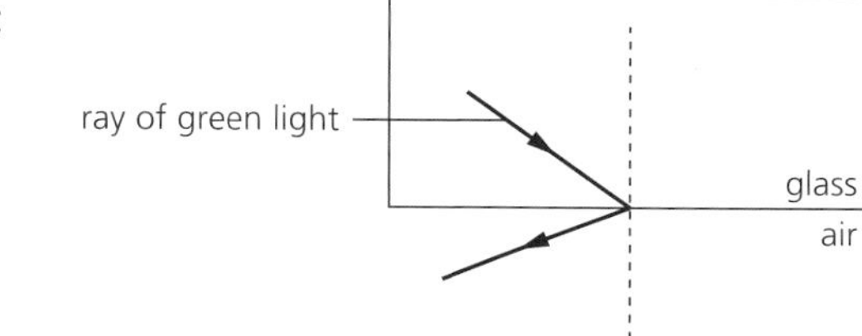

D

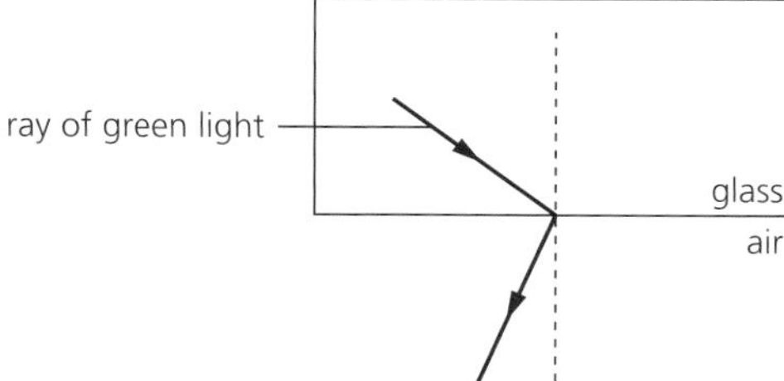

E

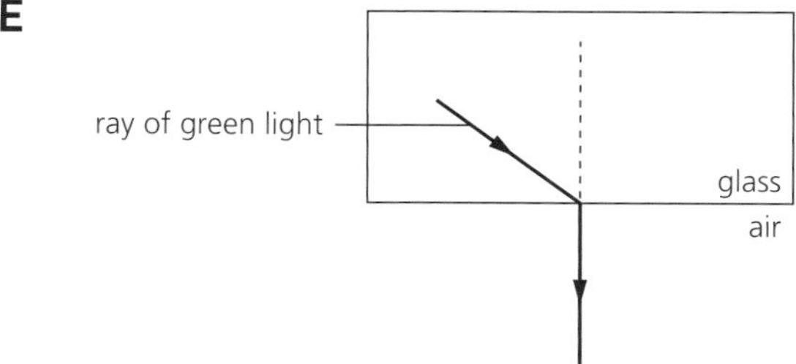

STUDENT MARGIN

CAS
W&R3.2
HTP
Page 65

STUDENT MARGIN

10 The activity of a radioactive source is 120 kBq.

The number of atoms that decay in 4 minutes is

A 480
B 500
C $2{\cdot}88 \times 10^4$
D $4{\cdot}80 \times 10^5$
E $2{\cdot}88 \times 10^7$.

CAS W&R4.2 HTP Page 73

11 A particular design of smoke detector contains a radioactive source.

The design specification for the radioactive source is:

- It should cause high ionisation of air over a distance of 3–5 cm.
- Its activity should remain high for at least 5 years.
- Its radiation should be absorbed by a plastic enclosure.

Which row in the table describes the most suitable source?

	Half-life	*Radiation emitted*
A	3 years	alpha
B	5 years	beta
C	3 minutes	gamma
D	29 years	beta
E	432 years	alpha

CAS W&R4.1 HTP Page 69

12 A worker in the nuclear industry received an equivalent dose of 0·08 μSv in 16 hours.

The equivalent dose rate is

A $1{\cdot}39 \times 10^{-12}\,\text{Sv h}^{-1}$
B $5{\cdot}0 \times 10^{-9}\,\text{Sv h}^{-1}$
C $1{\cdot}28 \times 10^{-6}\,\text{Sv h}^{-1}$
D $16{\cdot}08 \times 10^{-6}\,\text{Sv h}^{-1}$
E $4{\cdot}61 \times 10^{-3}\,\text{Sv h}^{-1}$.

CAS W&R4.7 HTP Page 71

13 Four tug boats are used to give a resultant force on a cruise ship as it enters a harbour.

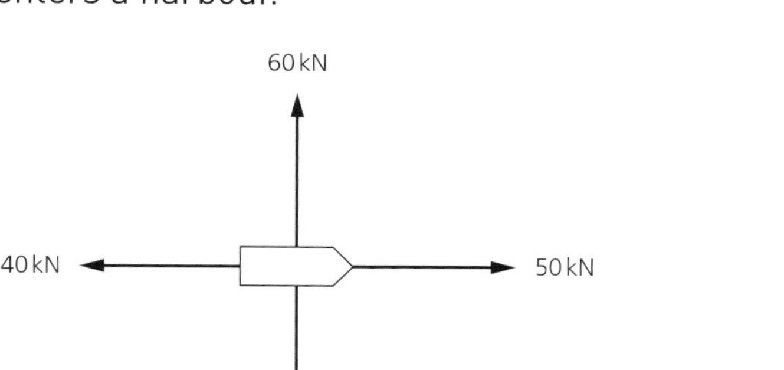

The forces applied by each boat are shown.

Which of the following forces could represent the resultant force on the cruise ship?

A

B 

C

D 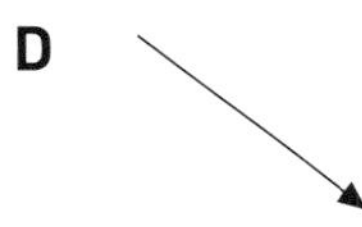

E

STUDENT MARGIN

CAS

D&S1.3

HTP

Page 83

14 The graph shows how the velocity of an object changes with time.

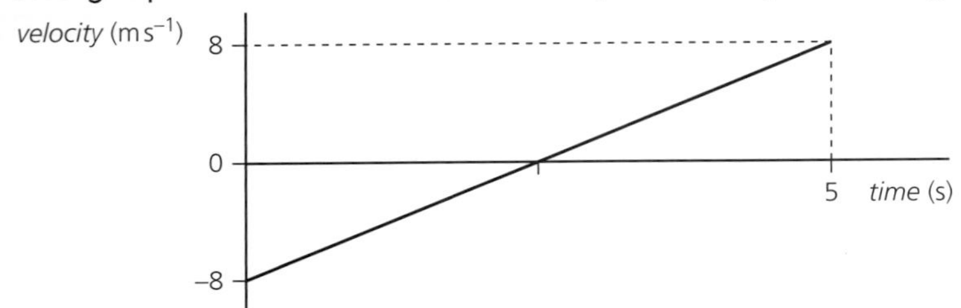

Which row in the table shows the displacement and acceleration of the object during the first 5 s?

	Displacement (m)	*Acceleration* (m s^{-2})
A	20	9·8
B	0	−9·8
C	20	3·2
D	0	−3·2
E	0	3·2

STUDENT MARGIN

CAS

D&S2.3

D&S3.2

HTP

Page 86

15 Two forces act on an 4 kg metal block as shown.

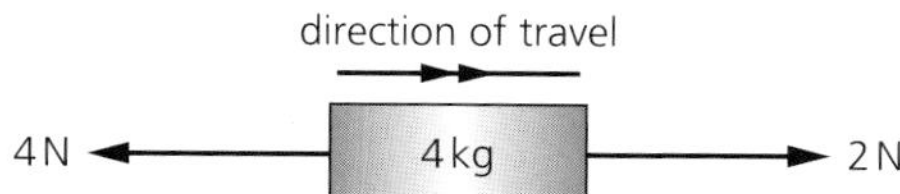

The block is initially moving at 4 m s^{-1} in the direction shown.

The speed–time graph for the block is

A

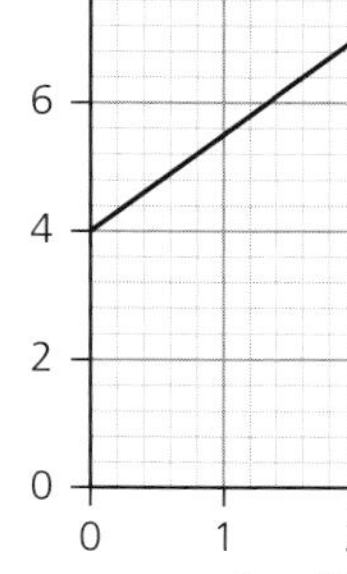

B

speed (m s^{-1}) 10 8 6 4 2 0; time (s) 0 1 2

C

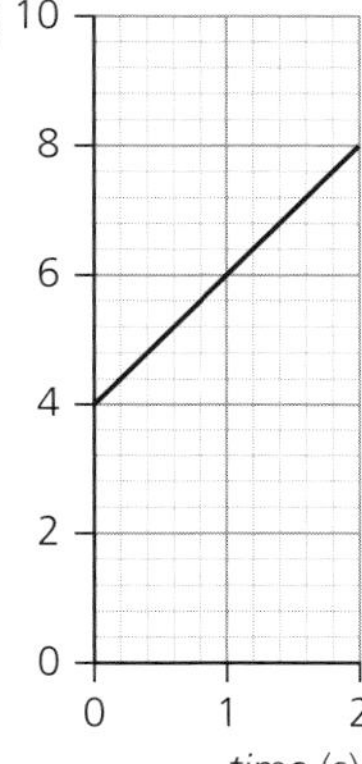

D

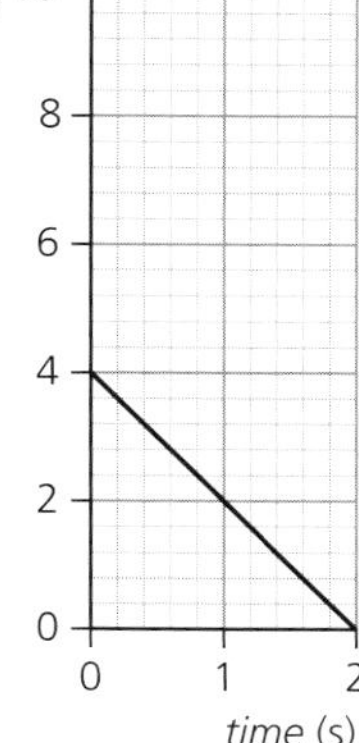

E

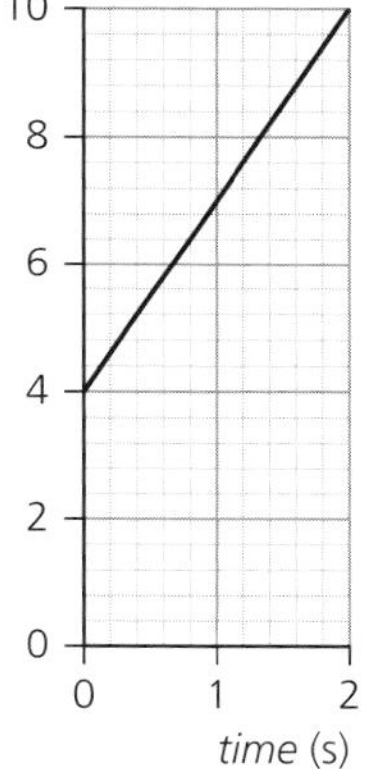

STUDENT MARGIN

CAS
D&S4.2
HTP
Page 96

16 The graph shows how the gravitational field strength varies with height above the Earth's surface.

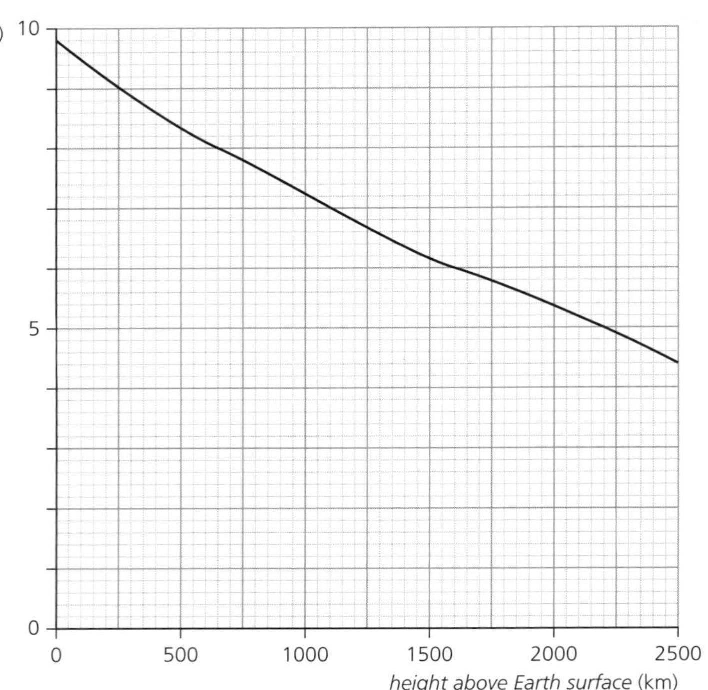

The International Space Station (ISS) orbits at 400 km above the Earth's surface. A British astronaut on board the ISS in orbit has a mass of 90 kg.

The weight of the astronaut while on board the ISS is

A 0 N
B 90 N
C 774 N
D 828 N
E 882 N.

STUDENT MARGIN

CAS
D&S4.4
HTP
Page 94

17 The Apollo 11 astronauts left the Moon in a space vehicle called the ascent module.

The ascent module had a mass of 5000 kg. At lift-off, the engine force was 15 000 N.

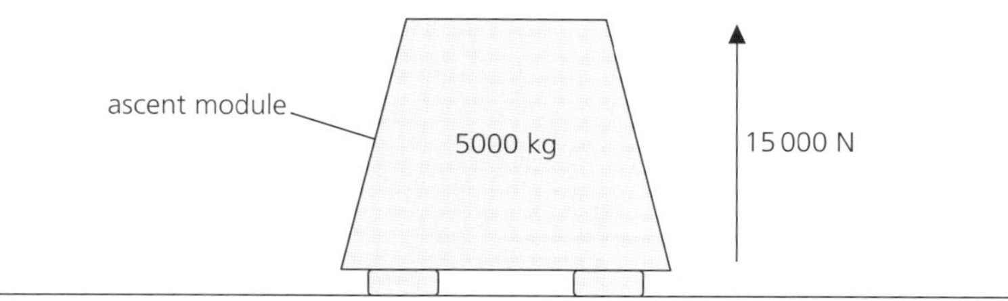

The acceleration of the module at lift-off was

A $1{\cdot}4\,m\,s^{-2}$
B $2{\cdot}0\,m\,s^{-2}$
C $3{\cdot}0\,m\,s^{-2}$
D $4{\cdot}6\,m\,s^{-2}$
E $6{\cdot}8\,m\,s^{-2}$.

18 An ascending space rocket's engines exert a downward force on exhaust gases when in flight.

Which of the following is the reaction to this force?

A The exhaust gases exert an upward force on the space rocket's engines.
B The Earth exerts an upward force on the space rocket's engines.
C The air in the atmosphere exerts an upward force on the space rocket's engines.
D The exhaust gases exert a downward force on the air in the atmosphere.
E The Earth exerts an upward force on the exhaust gases.

STUDENT MARGIN

CAS D&S4.5 HTP Page 94

CAS D&S4.6 HTP Page 95

19 In an experiment, two identical balls P and Q are projected horizontally from the edge of a table. The paths of the balls are shown below.

STUDENT MARGIN

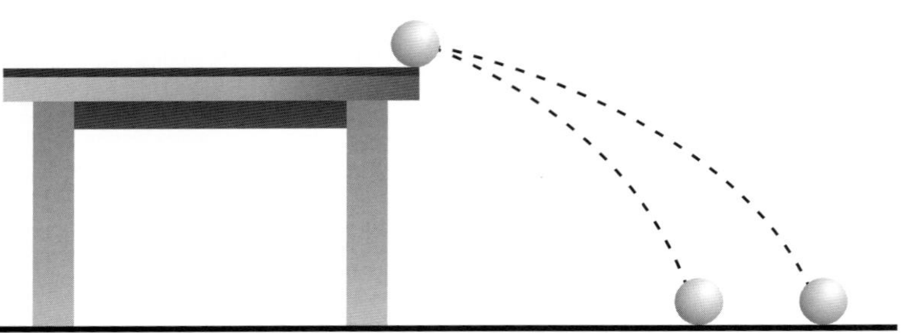

A student makes the following statements about the motion of the balls.

I The balls have different horizontal velocities.

II The balls take the same time to reach the floor.

III The balls have different final vertical velocities.

Which of the statements is/are correct?

A I only
B II only
C III only
D I and II only
E II and III only

CAS D&S5.1 HTP Page 104

20 The distance from the Sun to the nearest binary star is $4{\cdot}2 \times 10^{16}$ m.

This distance is equivalent to

A 0·5 light years
B 4·4 light years
C 106·5 light years
D 266·2 light years
E 1620 light years.

CAS D&S7.1 HTP Page 107

[END OF SECTION 1]

SECTION 2

SECTION 2 — 90 MARKS

Attempt ALL questions.

Reference may be made to the Data sheet on Page 36 of the question paper and to the Relationships sheet.

Care should be taken to give an appropriate number of significant figures in the final answers to calculations.

Write your answers clearly in the spaces provided in this paper. Any rough work must be written in this paper. You should score through your rough work when you have written your final copy.

Use **blue** or **black** ink.

MARKS | STUDENT MARGIN

1 A technician sets up an experiment to investigate the effect of an electric field on charged particles. An electric field is produced between two metal plates inside a container, at the top and bottom, and connected to a power supply.

Charged particles are placed inside the container and their movement recorded.

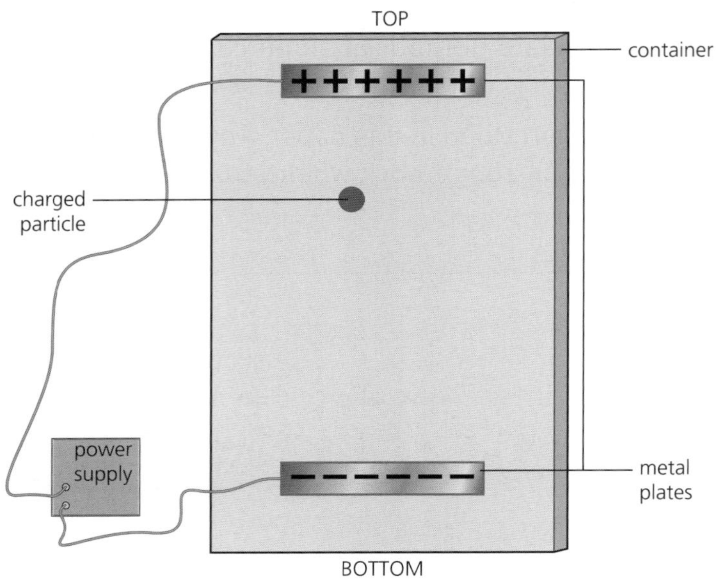

CAS E&E3.1 HTP Page 11

During one test, a charged particle is placed in the container.

The forces acting on the particle are shown in the diagram below.

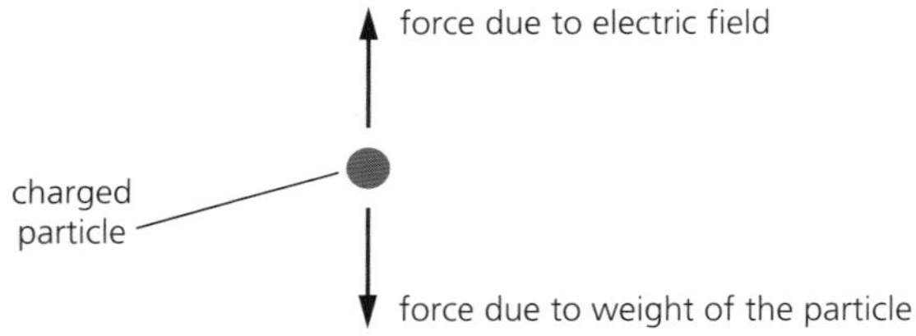

The particle remains stationary inside the electric field.

a) State the sign of the charge on the particle. 1

1 (continued)

MARKS	STUDENT MARGIN

b) The mass of the particle is $5{\cdot}4 \times 10^{-8}$ kg. Calculate the weight of the particle. 3

Space for working and answer

CAS
D&S4.4
HTP
Page 94

c) The electric field is switched off and the particle begins to fall. A velocity–time graph of the downward motion of the falling particle is shown below.

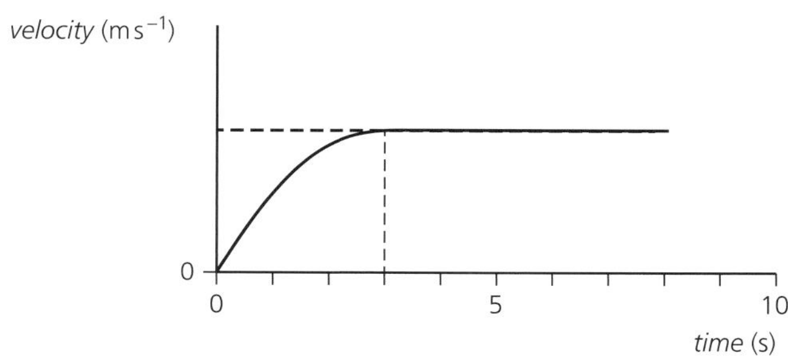

Describe and explain the movement of the particle after 3 s. 2

CAS
D&S4.1
HTP
Page 85

MARKS STUDENT MARGIN

2 A student investigates the resistance of a lamp. The student uses the circuit shown below to measure the current in the lamp at different voltages.

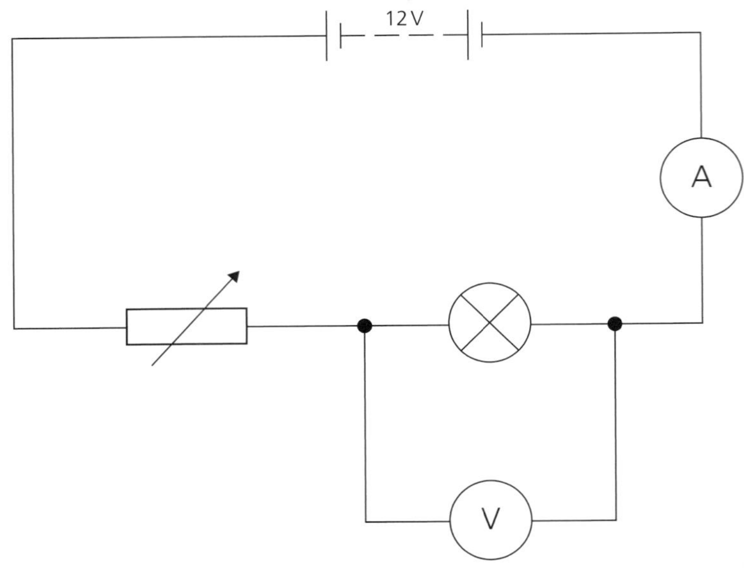

a) Explain how the current can be altered in this circuit. **1**

CAS E&E5.4 HTP Page 16

The student recorded the voltage across the lamp for different values of current in the lamp.

The table shows the student's results.

Voltage (V)	*Current* (A)
0	0
0·4	0·18
1·6	0·44
2·8	0·60
4·4	0·76
6·4	0·90
9·6	1·00

2 (continued)

b) (i) Using the graph paper below, draw a graph of these results

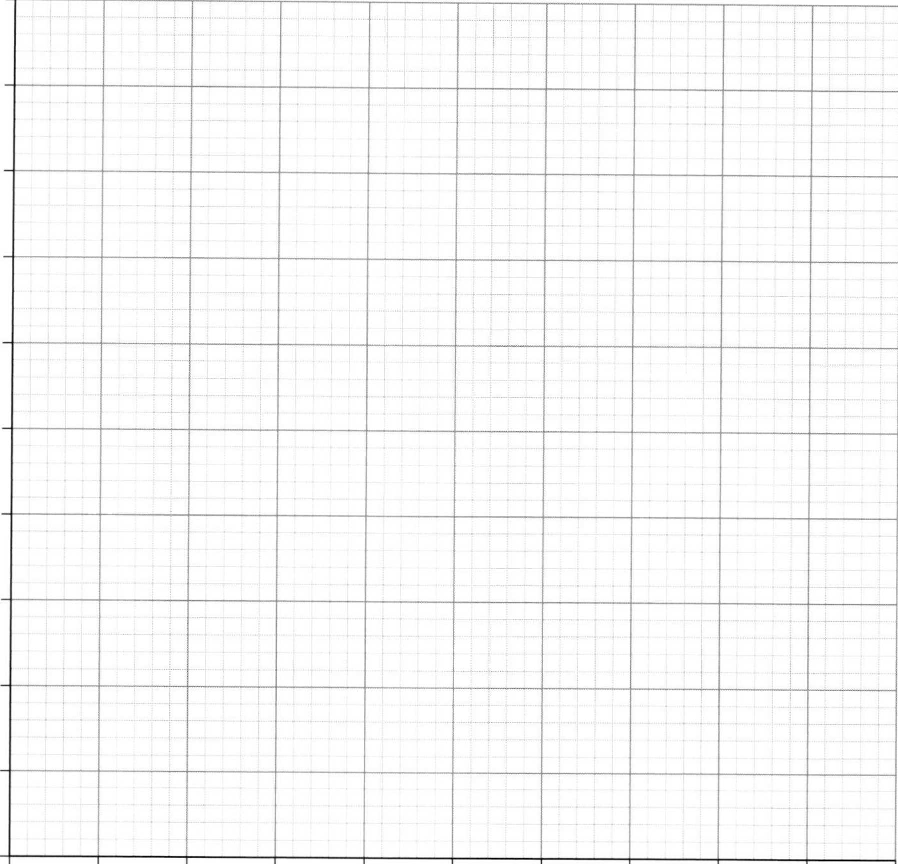

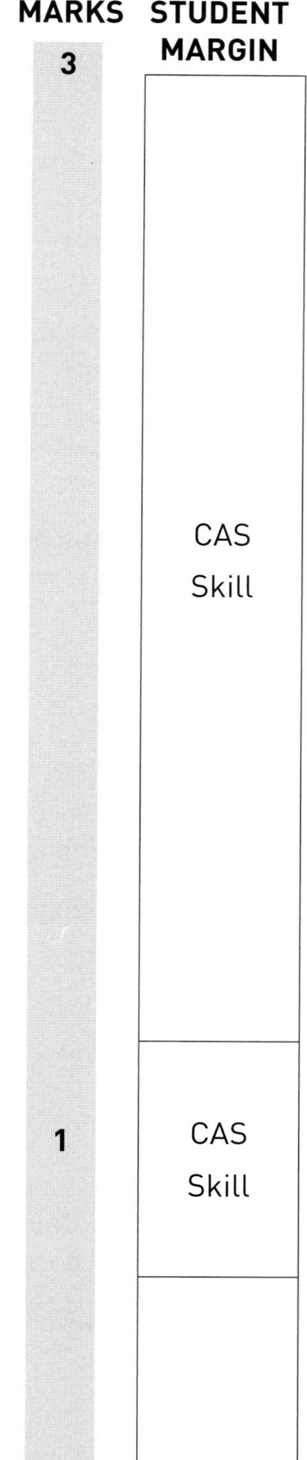

(ii) Use the graph to predict the value of the voltage across the lamp when the current in the lamp is 0·36 A.

(iii) Using information from the graph, state whether the resistance of the lamp filament **increases**, **stays the same** or **decreases** as the voltage increases.

You must **explain** your answer.

MARKS STUDENT MARGIN

3 Three new ceiling lamps are installed in a kitchen.

The lamps are connected to the mains in the circuit shown below.

CAS E&E5.4 HTP Page 17

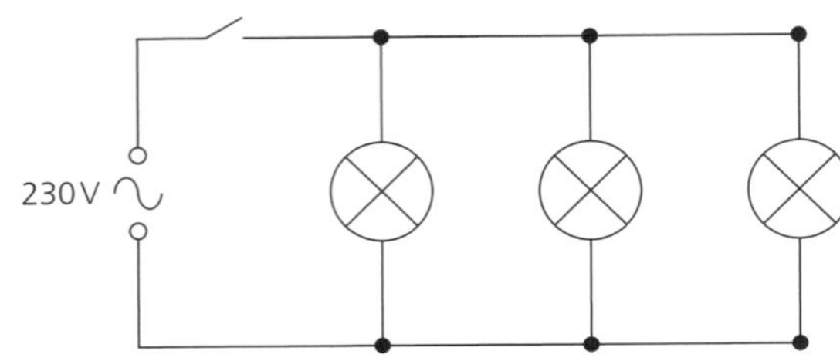

Each lamp is rated at 230 V, 50 W.

a) **(i)** Explain why the lamps must be connected in parallel. **1**

(ii) Calculate the resistance of each lamp when operating at their correct voltage. **3**

Space for working and answer

CAS E&E6.2 HTP Page 26

3 (continued)

MARKS	STUDENT MARGIN

b) Calculate the total current when all three lamps are operating. 3

Space for working and answer

CAS
E&E6.2
HTP
Page 26

MARKS STUDENT MARGIN

4 A student cooks vegetables using an electric steamer. Water in the base of the steamer is heated, causing steam to rise through holes in the base of two vegetable compartments. The steam cooks the vegetables.

The steamer has a rating of 800 W and is filled with 0·6 kg of water at a temperature of 25 °C.

a) Calculate the heat energy required to heat the water from 25 °C to its boiling point of 100 °C. **3** CAS E&E7.4 HTP Page 48

Space for working and answer

4 (continued)

	MARKS	STUDENT MARGIN
b) The vegetables need to be steamed for 12 minutes after the water has reached its boiling point of 100 °C. **(i)** Calculate the electrical energy supplied to the steamer during this time. *Space for working and answer*	3	CAS E&E6.1 HTP Page 26
(ii) Calculate the maximum mass of water that could be converted into steam in this time. *Space for working and answer*	3	CAS DS6.7 HTP Page 110
(iii) Explain why the mass calculated in part **b)(ii)** is the maximum mass of steam which can be produced.	1	CAS E&E1.1 HTP Page 8

MARKS STUDENT MARGIN

5 Scientists at a research station located in the Antarctic use a steel drum to store equipment.

The volume of the container is 0·25 m^3. The container has a lid which forms an airtight seal when attached to the container.

One empty container is left outside with the lid secured in position.

The pressure of the air inside the container is $1{\cdot}01 \times 10^5$ Pa. The temperature of the air inside the container is 10 °C.

During the night, the temperature of the air inside the container falls to −40 °C.

CAS E&E8.6 HTP Page 54

a) Calculate the air pressure inside the container at −40 °C. Assume that the volume of the container remains constant. **3**

Space for working and answer

5 (continued)

	MARKS	STUDENT MARGIN
b) The air pressure outside the container remains constant at $1{\cdot}01 \times 10^5$ Pa. **(i)** Calculate the pressure difference between the air outside and inside the container at −40 °C. *Space for working and answer*	1	CAS Skill
(ii) The surface area of the lid is $0{\cdot}45\,m^2$. Calculate the force on the lid due to the pressure difference. *Space for working and answer*	3	CAS E&E8.3 HTP Page 51
(iii) State the direction of this force on the lid.	1	CAS D&S1.3 HTP Page 51

MARKS STUDENT MARGIN

6 A student takes a dog for a walk at night in a field. The student can hear the dog barking in the distance ahead, but cannot see the dog in the beam of the torch.

Use your knowledge of physics to comment on why the student can hear the dog but cannot see the dog. 3

CAS
Skill
HTP
Page 82

MARKS STUDENT MARGIN

7 a) Explain the difference between alternating and direct current. 1

CAS
E&E2.3
HTP
Page 27

b) A student uses an oscilloscope, resistor and signal generator to investigate alternating current.

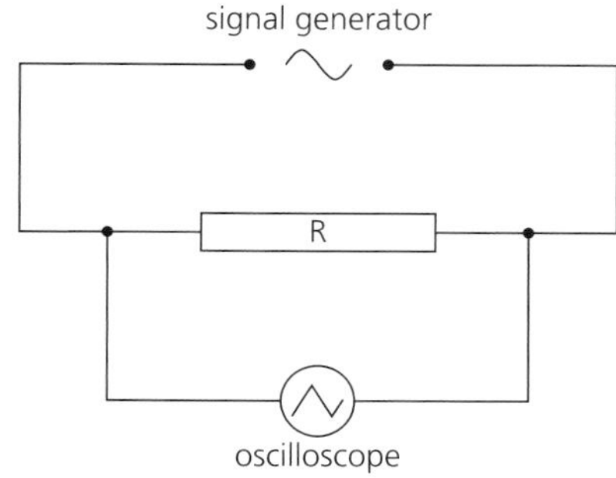

The signal generator produces an alternating voltage signal. The voltage and frequency of the signal can be varied.

The oscilloscope has controls which can be adjusted to allow the amplitude and period of an electrical voltage signal to be measured.

The following oscilloscope display was produced for one particular setting of voltage and frequency of the signal generator.

The voltage and time scale settings for the oscilloscope are shown. The oscilloscope grid is made up of 1 cm squares.

CAS
W&R1.2
HTP
Page 58

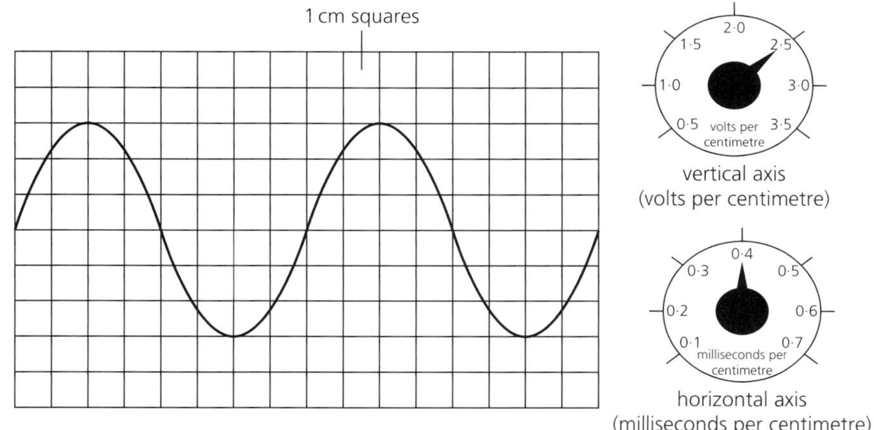

(i) What is the amplitude of the voltage supply? 1

7 b) (continued)

	MARKS	STUDENT MARGIN
(ii) What is the period of the wave?	1	CAS W&R1.2 HTP Page 58
(iii) Calculate the frequency of the wave. *Space for working and answer*	3	CAS W&R1.2 HTP Page 58

c) The student constructs the following circuits using LEDs connected to d.c. and a.c. power supplies.

CAS E&E5.2 HTP Page 43

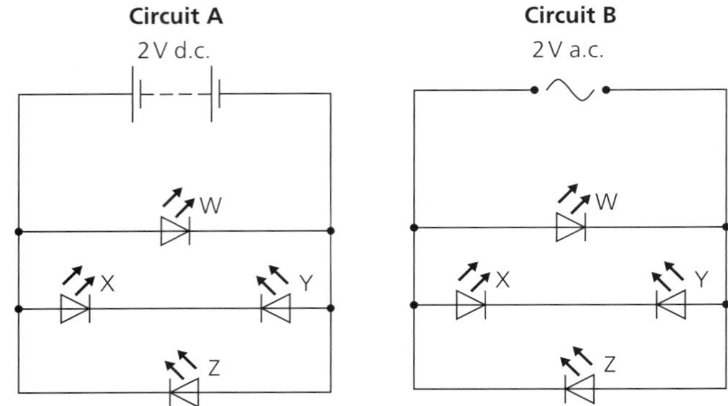

State which of the LEDs W, X, Y or Z will light:

(i) in circuit A? 1

(ii) in circuit B? 1

CAS E&E5.2 HTP Page 43

MARKS STUDENT MARGIN

8 The table lists three telescopes on satellites in orbit around the Earth which are used to monitor different bands of the electromagnetic spectrum of radiation detected from space.

Name of satellite	*Band of electromagnetic spectrum monitored*	*Approximate altitude above Earth* (km)
WISE	infrared	525
Chandra	X-rays	105 000
IRIS	ultraviolet	650

CAS W&R2.1 HTP Page 62

a) **(i)** List the satellites in order of increasing wavelength of the electromagnetic spectrum band monitored. **2**

1. ....

2. ....

3. ....

(ii) List the satellites in order of increasing period of orbit around the Earth. **2**

1. ....

2. ....

3. ....

CAS D&S6.3 HTP Page 105

8 (continued)

MARKS | STUDENT MARGIN

b) While monitoring signals from space, the IRIS satellite detects electromagnetic radiation with a wavelength of $2{\cdot}5 \times 10^{-7}$ m.

Calculate the frequency of the radiation. **3**

Space for working and answer

CAS W&R1.3 HTP Page 60

c) The Chandra satellite sends a radio signal to Earth. Calculate the time for the radio signal to reach Earth. **3**

Space for working and answer

CAS D&S1.5 HTP Page 79

d) Explain why telescopes on satellites in orbit around the Earth are required to monitor some electromagnetic radiation from space, in addition to Earth-based telescopes. **1**

CAS W&R2.1 HTP Page 113

MARKS | STUDENT MARGIN

9 Currently, nuclear power stations use nuclear fission as the source of energy for the production of electricity. During the fission process, an atomic particle is absorbed by a uranium nucleus. Fission products and neutrons are produced.

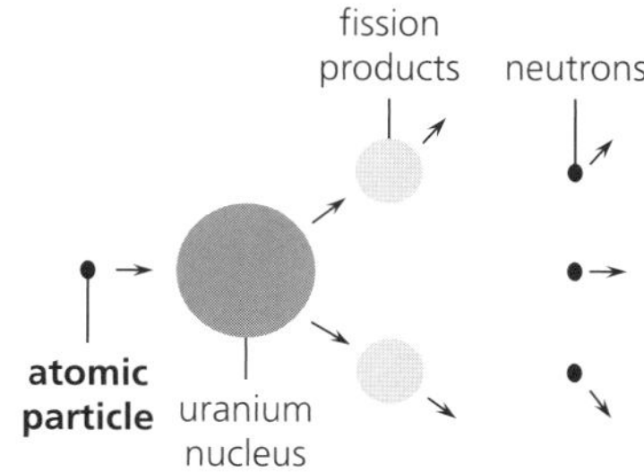

CAS W&R4.11 HTP Page 75

a) Name the atomic particle absorbed by the uranium nucleus during nuclear fission. **1**

b) During research of the fission process, a graph was produced showing the activity against time for a sample of one of the fission products.

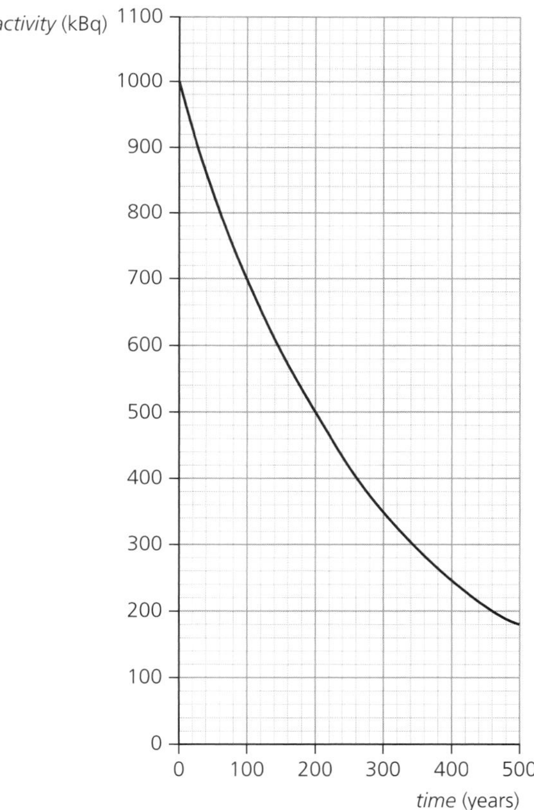

CAS W&R4.10 HTP Page 74

(i) Determine the half-life of the fission product. **1**

9 b) (continued) | MARKS | STUDENT MARGIN

(ii) The safe level of activity for this sample is 62·5 kBq.

Calculate the time taken for the activity of this sample to fall to this level. **2**

Space for working and answer

CAS W&R4.10 HTP Page 74

c) Some nuclear power stations have reached the end of their predicted lifetime of operation and must be dismantled.

During the dismantling process workers are regularly monitored for exposure to radiation.

A demolition worker of mass 70 kg was found to have been exposed to a radioactive source emitting alpha particles.

Across the whole body, the worker absorbed 850 μJ of energy.

(i) Calculate the absorbed dose received by the worker. **3**

Space for working and answer

CAS W&R4.4 HTP Page 71

STUDENT MARGIN

5 Which is the correct symbol for a light-dependent resistor (LDR)?

A

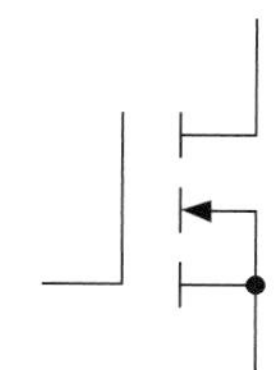

B

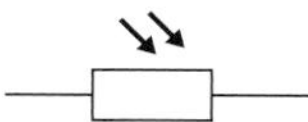

C

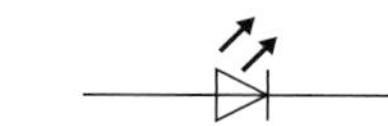

D

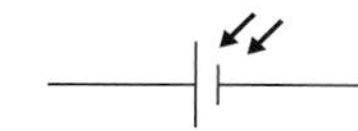

E

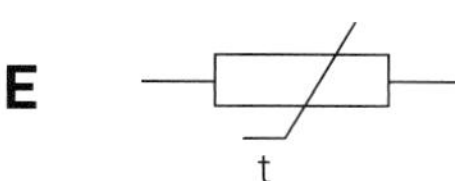

CAS E&E5.2 HTP Page 41

6 A lorry sidelight bulb rated at 48 W has a current of 2 A when operating at its correct rating.

Which row in the table shows the resistance of its filament and the voltage across the bulb when it is operating at the correct rating?

	Resistance of the filament (Ω)	*Voltage across the bulb* (V)
A	12	24
B	12	96
C	24	24
D	192	24
E	192	96

CAS E&E6.2 HTP Page 26

STUDENT MARGIN

7 Which graph represents the correct relationship between the pressure p and the volume V of a fixed mass of gas at constant temperature?

A

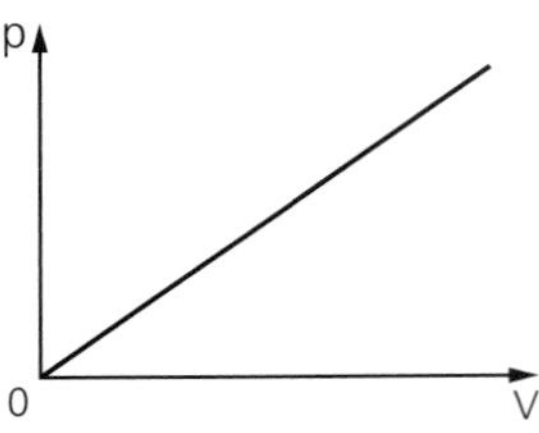

B

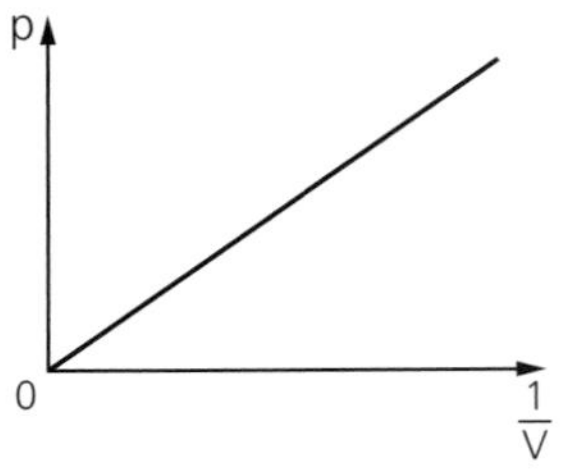

C

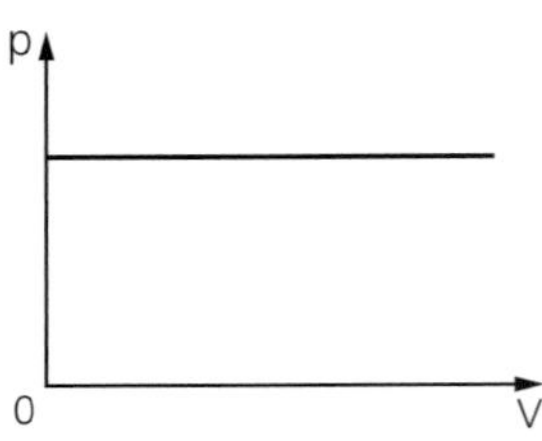

D

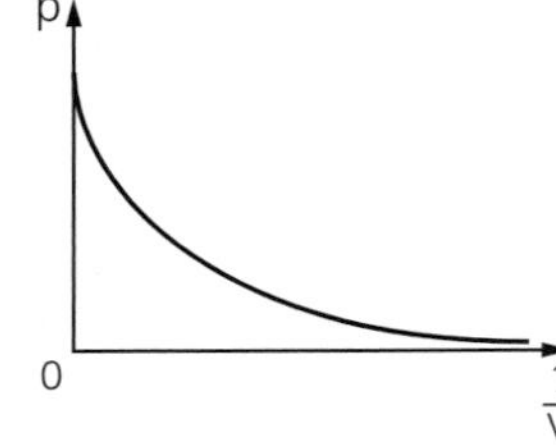

E

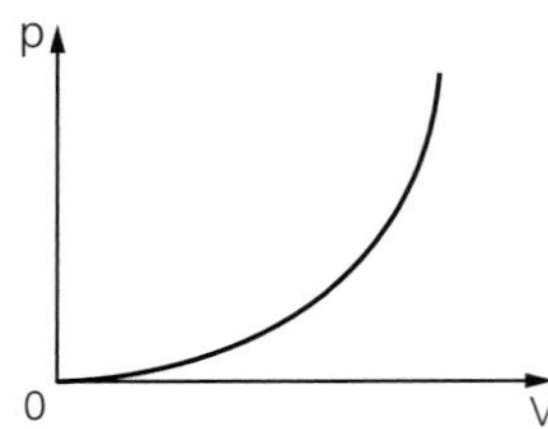

CAS
E&E8.6
HTP
Page 53

STUDENT MARGIN

8 A ray of white light passes from air into glass.

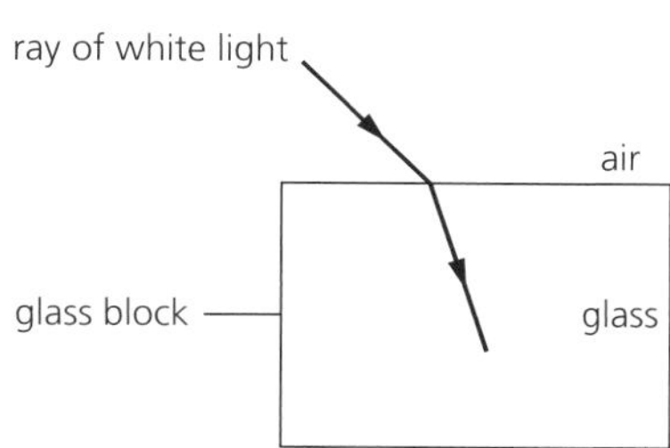

Which row in the table correctly shows the effect on the wave speed, frequency and wavelength of the light when it enters the glass?

	Wave speed	*Frequency*	*Wavelength*
A	decreases	increases	constant
B	increases	constant	decreases
C	constant	increases	increases
D	decreases	constant	decreases
E	decreases	increases	constant

CAS W&R3.2 HTP Page 65

9 A radioactive source emits alpha, beta and gamma radiation. A detector, connected to a counter, is placed 10 mm in front of the source. The counter records 500 counts per minute.

A 5 mm sheet of aluminium is placed between the source and the detector. The counter now records 50 counts per minute.

The radiation now detected by the detector is

A alpha only
B alpha and beta only
C beta only
D beta and gamma only
E gamma only.

CAS W&R4.1 HTP Page 69

10 For a particular radioactive source, 30 000 atoms decay in a time of 5 minutes.

The activity of this source is

A $1{\cdot}7 \times 10^{-4}$ Bq
B $0{\cdot}01$ Bq
C 100 Bq
D $1{\cdot}5 \times 10^{5}$ Bq
E $9{\cdot}0 \times 10^{6}$ Bq.

CAS W&R4.2 HTP Page 73

STUDENT MARGIN

11 A tissue sample of mass 0·08 kg is exposed to 2 mJ of beta radiation.

The absorbed dose received by the tissue is

A 0·025 Gy
B 25·0 Gy
C 40·0 Gy
D 160·0 Gy
E $2{\cdot}5 \times 10^4$ Gy.

CAS W&R4.4 HTP Page 70

12 A sample of tissue receives an absorbed dose of 50 mGy when exposed to slow neutrons.

The equivalent dose is

A $1{\cdot}5 \times 10^{-5}$ Sv
B 0·15 Sv
C 0·5 Sv
D 150 Sv
E 500 Sv.

CAS W&R4.4 HTP Page 71

13 When considering the exposure of humans to radiation, the *effective equivalent dose* is used to assess the potential for long-term effects of radiation exposure that might occur in the future.

Which row in the table correctly shows the current annual safe limits of effective equivalent dose for members of the public and for employees?

	Members of public and employees under 18	*Employees over 18*
A	20 mSv	1 mSv
B	100 mSv	20 mSv
C	20 mSv	100 mSv
D	1 mSv	1 mSv
E	1 mSv	20 mSv

CAS W&R4.6 HTP Page 71

STUDENT MARGIN

14 Which of the following contains two scalar quantities and one vector quantity?

A Displacement, velocity, acceleration
B Speed, velocity, displacement
C Time, distance, force
D Acceleration, mass, displacement
E Displacement, force, velocity

CAS D&S1.2 HTP Page 78

15 An athlete sprints 50 m South then 30 m North in 8 seconds.

Which row in the table shows the average speed and average velocity of the athlete?

	Average speed ($m\,s^{-1}$)	*Average velocity* ($m\,s^{-1}$)
A	2·5	2·5 North
B	2·5	10 South
C	10	2·5 North
D	10	2·5 South
E	10	10 South

CAS D&S1.5 HTP Page 79

16 The graph shows how the velocity of an object changes with time.

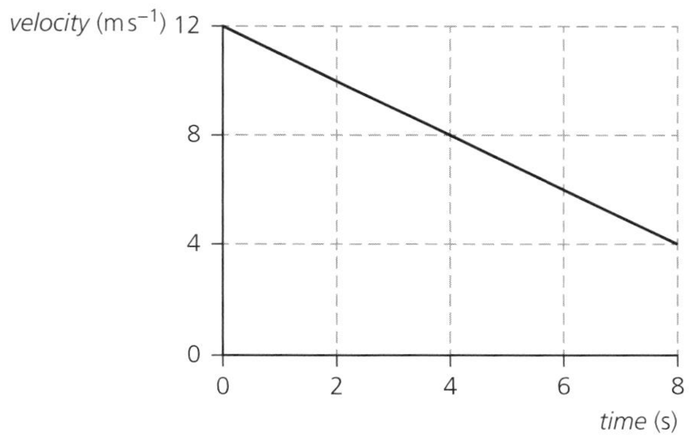

The acceleration of the object is

A $-1\,m\,s^{-2}$
B $1\,m\,s^{-2}$
C $-2\,m\,s^{-2}$
D $2\,m\,s^{-2}$
E $24\,m\,s^{-2}$.

CAS D&S3.2 HTP Page 80

STUDENT MARGIN

17 A 1 kg ball is dropped into a deep well. The graph shows the speed of the ball from the instant of its release in air until it has fallen several metres through the water towards the bottom of the well.

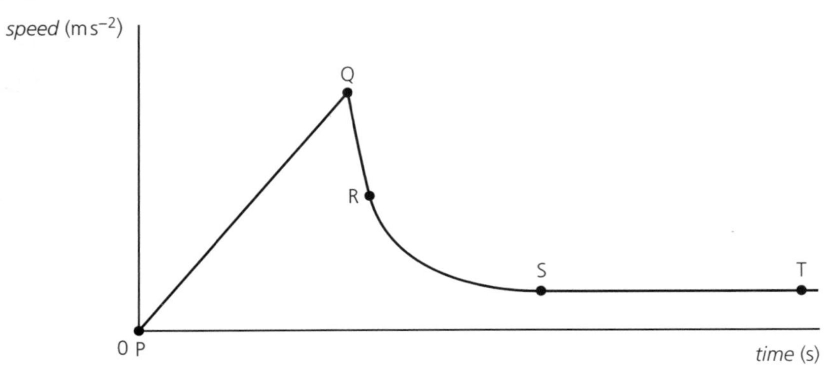

Which part of the graph shows when the ball was experiencing a constant downward force of 9·8 N?

A PQ only
B QR only
C RS only
D ST only
E PT

CAS
D&S4.1
HTP
Page 91

18 Two identical balls X and Y are projected horizontally from the edge of a cliff.

The path taken by each ball is shown.

The effects of air resistance can be ignored.

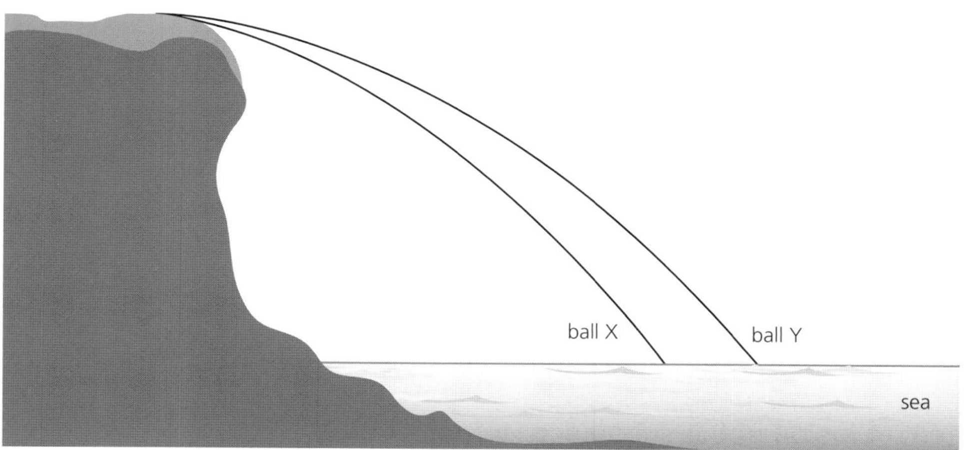

A student makes the following statements about the motion of the two balls.

I They take different times to reach sea level.
II They have a horizontal acceleration.
III They have different horizontal velocities.

Which of these statements is/are correct?

A I only
B II only
C III only
D I and II only
E I and III only

STUDENT MARGIN

CAS
D&S5.1
HTP
Page 104

19 A solid substance of mass 0·25 kg is placed in an insulated container and heated continuously by a 200 W heater.

The graph shows how the temperature of the substance changes in time.

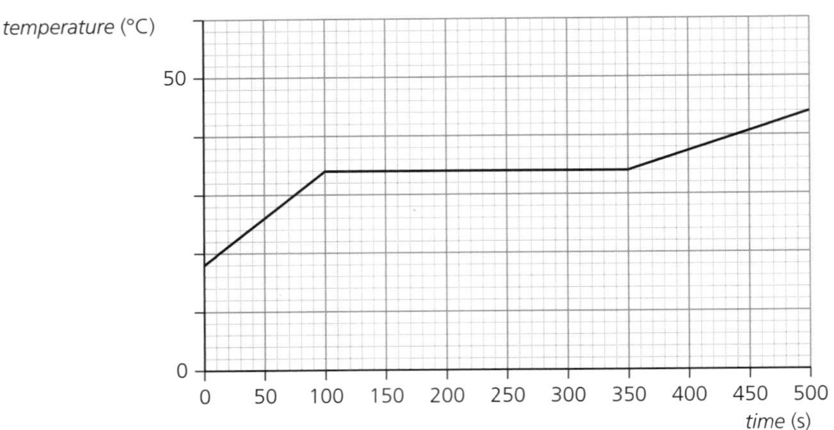

The specific latent heat of fusion of the substance is

A $5 \cdot 0\ \text{J kg}^{-1}$

B $8 \cdot 0 \times 10^{4}\ \text{J kg}^{-1}$

C $1 \cdot 2 \times 10^{5}\ \text{J kg}^{-1}$

D $2 \cdot 0 \times 10^{5}\ \text{J kg}^{-1}$

E $4 \cdot 0 \times 10^{4}\ \text{J kg}^{-1}$.

STUDENT MARGIN

CAS

D&S6.7

HTP

Page 110

STUDENT MARGIN

20 A line spectrum obtained from a distant star is shown below.

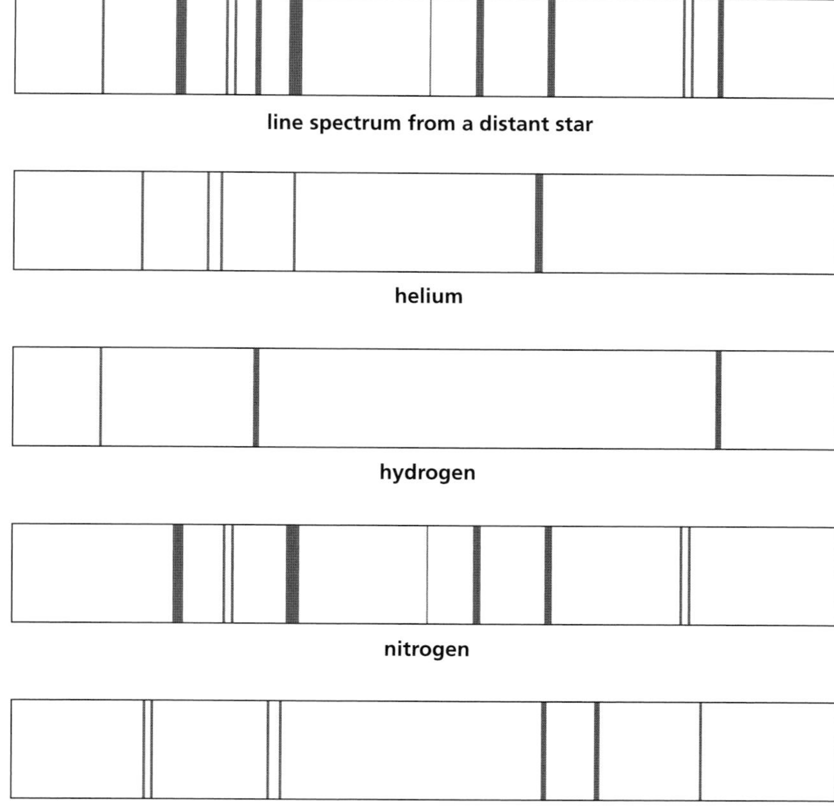

The two elements present in the star are

A helium and nitrogen
B hydrogen and argon
C helium and argon
D helium and hydrogen
E hydrogen and nitrogen.

CAS
D&S7.5
HTP
Page 114

[END OF SECTION 1]

SECTION 2

SECTION 2 — 90 MARKS

Attempt ALL questions.

Reference may be made to the Data sheet on Page 74 of the question paper and to the Relationships sheet.

Care should be taken to give an appropriate number of significant figures in the final answers to calculations.

Write your answers clearly in the spaces provided in this paper. Any rough work must be written in this paper. You should score through your rough work when you have written your final copy.

Use **blue** or **black** ink.

MARKS STUDENT MARGIN

1 A city in Europe is famous for its water fountain situated in a lake.

Every second, water pumps force 500 kg of water out of a vertical nozzle at a speed of $55\ m\ s^{-1}$.

CAS
E&E1.3
HTP
Page 100

a) Calculate the kinetic energy of this water as it emerges from the nozzle. **3**

Space for working and answer

b) Show that the maximum height that the 500 kg of water could reach is 155 m. **3**

Space for working and answer

CAS
E&E1.2
HTP
Page 100

c) In practice, the water jet reaches a height of 140 m instead of 155 m. State the reason for this difference. **1**

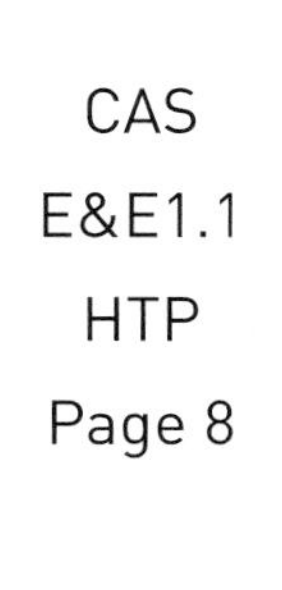

MARKS STUDENT MARGIN

2 A student decides to construct an electronic egg timer.

The student connects a capacitor in the following circuit.

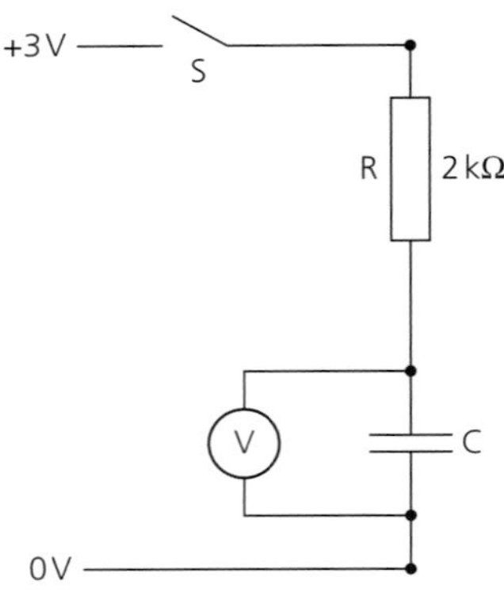

The voltage across the capacitor is measured by a voltmeter.

When switch S is open the voltmeter reading is zero. The switch is now closed.

A graph of the voltmeter readings against time is shown.

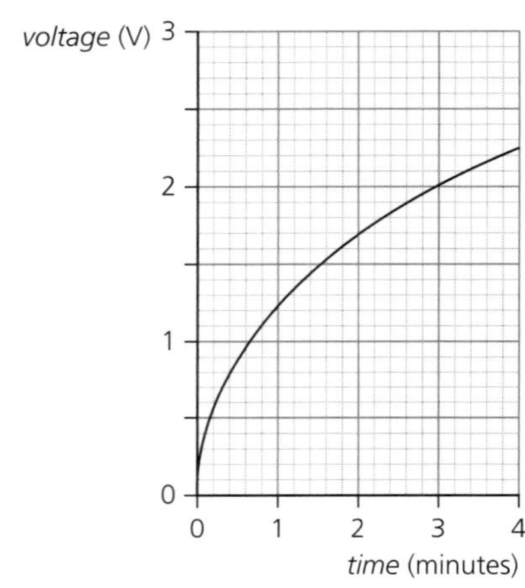

CAS E&E5.2 HTP Page 34

a) **(i)** State the voltage across the capacitor after 3 minutes. **1**

(ii) Explain why the current in R is not constant after switch S is closed. **1**

CAS E&E5.2 HTP Page 33

2 a) (continued) | MARKS | STUDENT MARGIN

(iii) Calculate the current in R after 3 minutes. **4**

Space for working and answer

CAS E&E4.2 HTP Page 33

b) The circuit is now connected to a switching circuit to operate a buzzer.

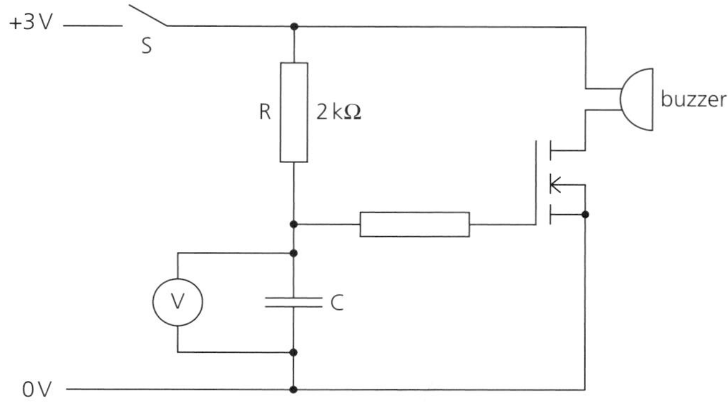

Explain how the circuit operates to make the buzzer sound. **2**

CAS E&E5.3 HTP Page 46

MARKS STUDENT MARGIN

3 A house has a solar heat exchanger and a solar cell array installed on its roof.

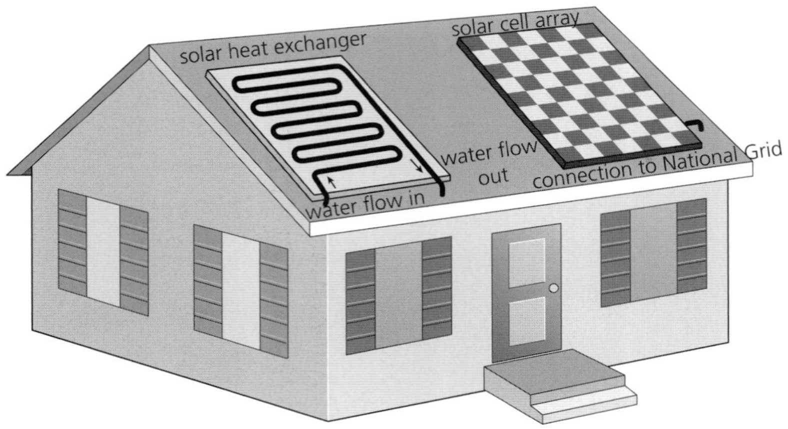

Solar heat exchanger	*Solar cell array*
Water is pumped into the solar heat exchanger, where heat energy from the sun raises its temperature. The heated water continues to a separate heat exchanger inside the house where the energy is stored for later use.	The solar cell array converts solar energy into electrical energy where it is connected and supplied to the National Grid. The householder is paid for the electrical energy supplied.

The householder decided to compare the outputs of the solar heat exchanger and the solar cell array.

The solar heat exchanger and solar cell array were tested over 5 hours on a sunny day.

The following results were recorded.

Solar heat exchanger	
average water temperature **in** (°C)	15·5
average water temperature **out** (°C)	25·8
mass of water heated during 5 hours (kg)	250·0

Solar cell array	
average output power during 5 hours (W)	350

3 **(continued)**

		MARKS	STUDENT MARGIN
a)	Calculate the solar energy transferred into heat energy by the solar heat exchanger during the five hours. *Space for working and answer*	3	CAS E&E7.4 HTP Page 49
b)	Calculate how long it would take, in hours, for the solar cell array to supply the equivalent amount of heat energy produced by the solar heat exchanger in part **a**). *Space for working and answer*	3	CAS E&E6.1 HTP Page 26

MARKS STUDENT MARGIN

4 A car engine manufacturer tests a diesel engine. Diesel engines have cylinders filled with air. A piston is used to compress the air, causing an increase in its temperature.

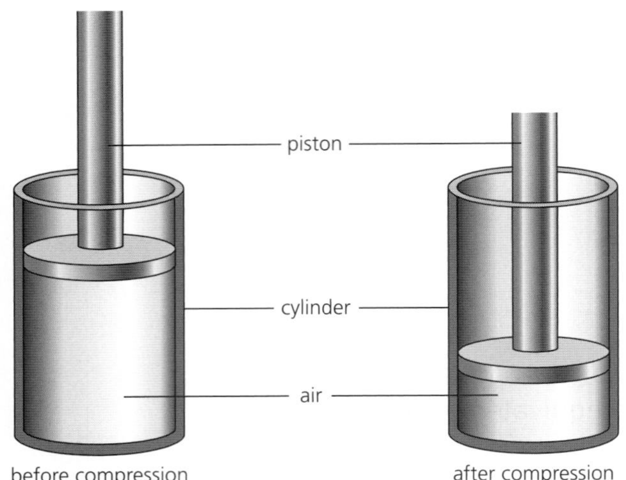

During one test the manufacturer obtained the following results.

	Before compression	*After compression*
Volume of air in cylinder (m^3)	$5{\cdot}0 \times 10^{-4}$	$2{\cdot}0 \times 10^{-5}$
Pressure of air in cylinder (Pa)	$1{\cdot}0 \times 10^{5}$	$5{\cdot}0 \times 10^{6}$
Temperature of air in cylinder (°C)	20·0	

CAS E&E8.6 HTP Page 56

a) Calculate the final temperature of the air in the cylinder after compression. **3**

Space for working and answer

4 (continued)

b) After compression, fuel is injected into the compressed air.

MARKS | STUDENT MARGIN

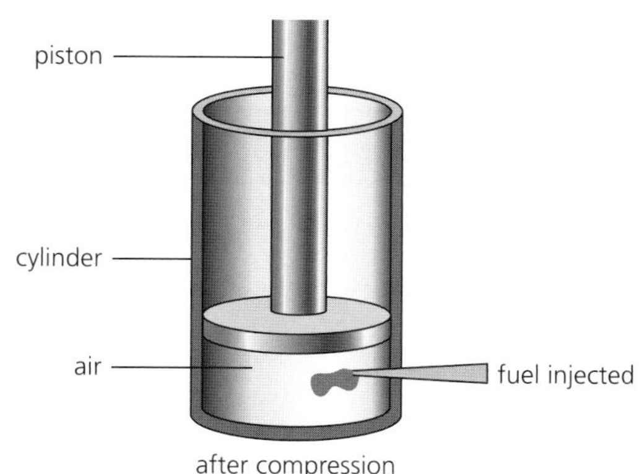

after compression

The fuel ignites, causing combustion. This causes the pressure inside the cylinder to increase to $7{\cdot}0 \times 10^6$ Pa. The pressure of air outside the cylinder is $1{\cdot}0 \times 10^5$ Pa. The surface area of the piston is $6{\cdot}4 \times 10^{-3}\,m^2$.

(i) Show that the force exerted on the piston is $4{\cdot}4 \times 10^4$ N. **3**

Space for working and answer

CAS E&E8.3 HTP Page 51

(ii) This force causes the piston to be pushed upwards, resulting in an increase in the volume of the air in the piston.

Explain in terms of the kinetic mode of gases why the pressure of the air inside the piston is reduced as the piston moves upwards. **1**

CAS E&E8.5 HTP Page 56

MARKS STUDENT MARGIN

5 In a leisure swimming pool a wave machine produces water waves that travel across the pool. The waves are viewed from above.

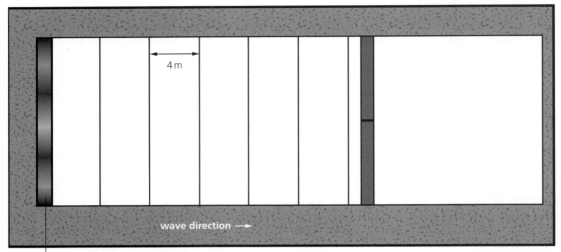

4 m

wave direction →

wave machine

During one operation of the machine, waves of wavelength 4 m are produced at a frequency of 0·25 Hz.

a) **(i)** Calculate the period of the waves. **3**

Space for working and answer

CAS W&R1.3 HTP Page 59

(ii) Calculate the speed of the waves. **3**

Space for working and answer

CAS W&R1.3 HTP Page 60

5 a) (continued)

	MARKS	STUDENT MARGIN

The swimming pool has barriers which can be opened to extend the pool.

The barriers are opened to leave a 2 m gap.

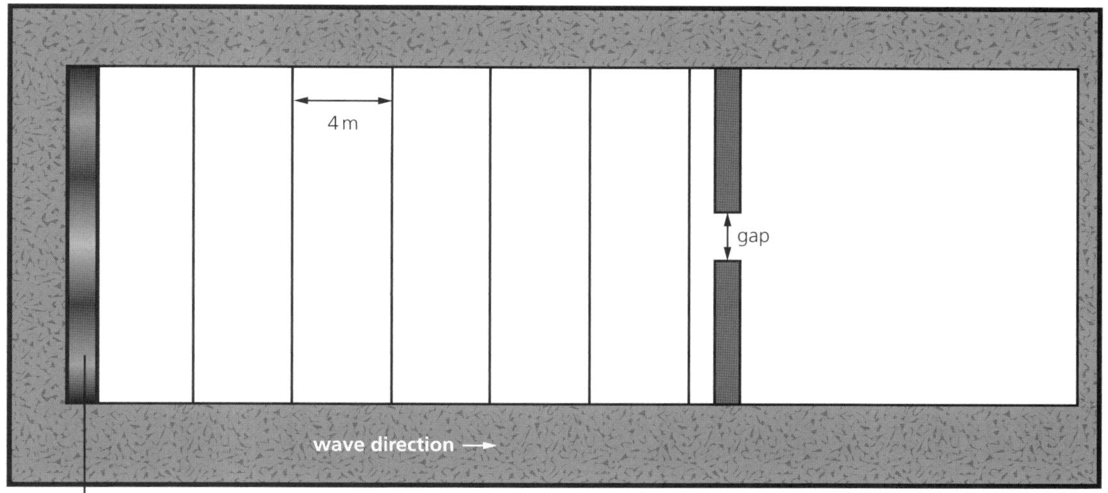

(iii) Complete the diagram to show the wave pattern on the right-hand side of the gap. **2**

CAS W&R1.4 HTP Page 60

b) At a swimming competition, an underwater camera is used to view the competitors as they swim.

The underwater camera films a swimmer standing on the box outside the pool, waiting to start the race.

Complete the diagram to show the path of a ray of light from the swimmer to the camera.

You should include a normal in your diagram. **3**

CAS W&R3.2 HTP Page 66

MARKS | STUDENT MARGIN

6 a) The diagram shows the electromagnetic spectrum.

gamma rays	X-rays	ultraviolet rays	visible light		microwaves	radio waves

(i) Name the missing radiation. **1**

CAS W&R2.1 HTP Page 62

(ii) State a detector of X–rays. **1**

CAS W&R2.2 HTP Page 64

(iii) Which radiation band has the lowest energy? **1**

CAS W&R2.1 HTP Page 62

(iv) Which radiation band has the highest frequency? **1**

CAS D&S7.1 HTP Page 107

b) Scientists used telescopes to detect microwaves from the Andromeda galaxy.

The galaxy was estimated to be $2{\cdot}4 \times 10^{22}$ m from Earth.

Determine this distance in light years. **3**

Space for working and answer

CAS W&R1.5 HTP Page 60

6 (continued)

MARKS STUDENT MARGIN

c) Before satellite communication was common, commercial shipping around the world received weather forecasts from land-based radio transmitters. Radio signals were broadcast on extremely long wavelengths.

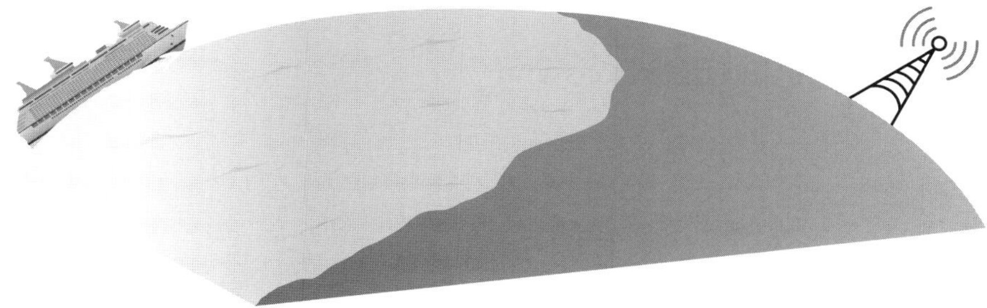

CAS D&S1.5 HTP Page 59

(i) Suggest why such long wavelengths were used to broadcast the shipping weather forecasts. **1**

(ii) One such radio transmitter broadcast using a radio signal of wavelength 1500 m. The signal took 0·0046 s to reach a ship on the ocean.

Calculate the distance of the ship from the transmitter. **3**

Space for working and answer

CAS D&S1.5 HTP Page 79

MARKS STUDENT MARGIN

7 Knowledge of the properties of waves in the electromagnetic spectrum has led to the development of many medical procedures for diagnosing and treating illnesses.

Use your knowledge of physics to comment on some of the developments.

Make reference to typical sources and detectors and applications in your answer. 3

CAS

Skill

MARKS STUDENT MARGIN

8 A technician conducted an experiment to determine the half-life of a radioactive source. The apparatus used is shown.

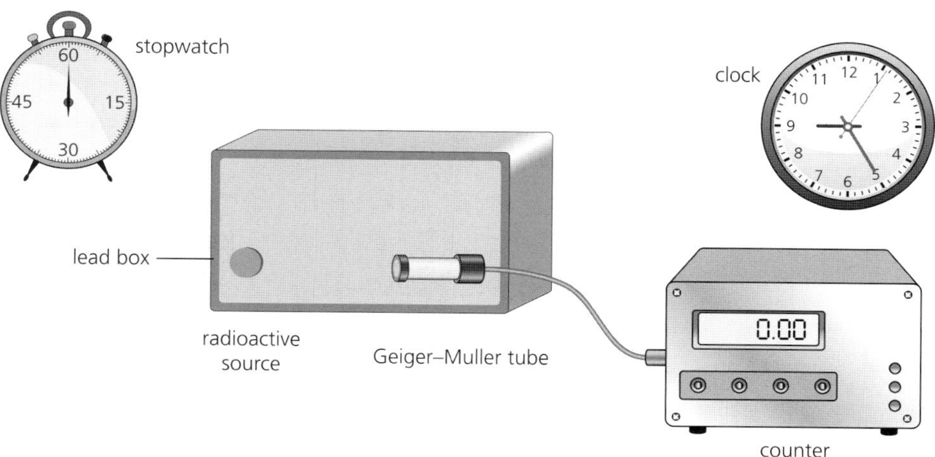

The source and detector were placed in a lead box.

a) Suggest why the experiment was carried out inside a lead box. **1**

CAS W&R4.3 HTP Page 70

b) The graph displays the data from the experiment.

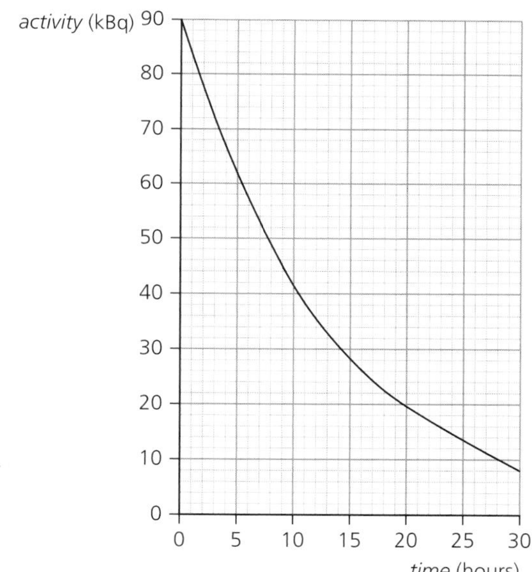

(i) What is meant by the term *half-life*? **1**

CAS W&R4.9 HTP Page 73

(ii) Use information from the graph to determine the half-life. **1**

CAS W&R4.10 HTP Page 74

	MARKS	STUDENT MARGIN

8 (continued)

c) A radioisotope was delivered to a hospital for use as a tracer in patients.

(i) While being transported to the hospital, the small box containing the radioisotope was positioned in the middle of a very large container.

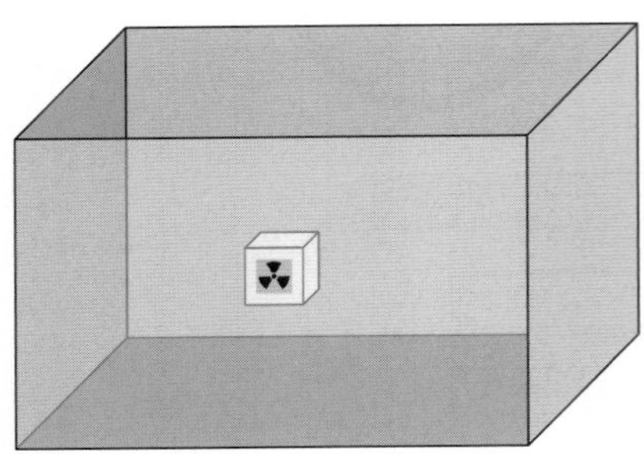

Suggest a reason for this.

You must explain your answer. **2** CAS W&R4.1 HTP Page 69

(ii) The activity of the radioisotope on delivery was 800 kBq at 7am 5th July.

The half-life of the radioisotope is 8 hours.

The advice stated that the radioisotope should not be used if the activity has fallen below 100 kBq.

A radiologist wanted to use the radioisotope at 11am 6th July.

Determine whether the radiologist should use the radioisotope. **2** CAS W&R4.10 HTP Page 74

Space for working and answer

MARKS STUDENT MARGIN

9 A passenger aircraft of mass 360 000 kg prepares for take-off.

The speed–time graph for the aircraft's motion on the runway from rest until it takes off is shown.

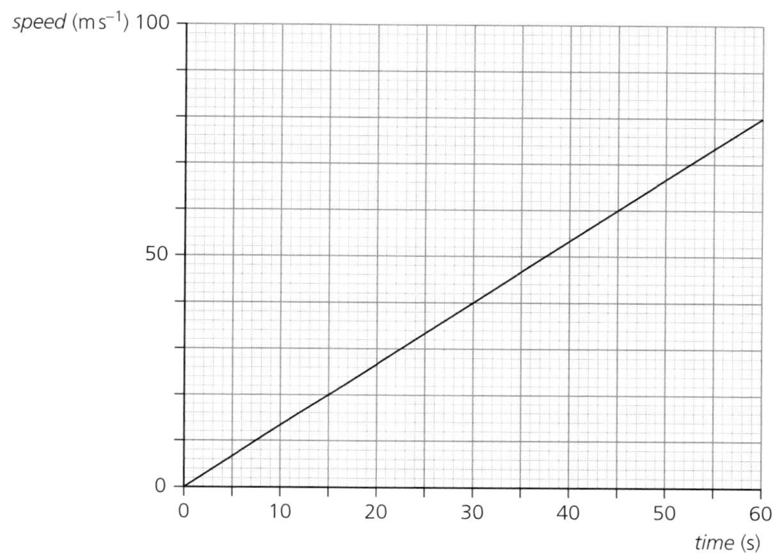

CAS D&S3.2 HTP Page 86

a) **(i)** Calculate the acceleration of the aircraft during take-off. **3**

Space for working and answer

	MARKS	STUDENT MARGIN
9 a) (continued)		
(ii) The forward force produced by the aircraft engines is 500 kN. Calculate the average frictional force acting on the aircraft during take-off. *Space for working and answer*	4	CAS D&S4.2 HTP Page 96
(iii) Calculate the length of runway required by the aircraft for take-off. *Space for working and answer*	3	CAS D&S2.3 HTP Page 85

9) (continued)

	MARKS	STUDENT MARGIN
b) During the flight, the aircraft flies at a constant speed and height.		

Calculate the upward force acting on the aircraft. **3** — CAS D&S4.1 HTP Page 96

Space for working and answer

c) When flying an aircraft between London and New York, an airline pilot is exposed to cosmic radiation at an equivalent dose rate of 8 μSv h^{-1}. Each flight lasts 7 hours. The pilot makes 106 of these flights in one year.

Calculate the equivalent dose received by the pilot from this exposure in one year. **3** — CAS W&R4.7 HTP Page 71

Space for working and answer

C

MARKS STUDENT MARGIN

10 Sir Isaac Newton described three laws of motion.

For each of these laws, describe an example of the law in use during everyday life. **3**

CAS Skill

11 The exploration vehicle Curiosity landed on the planet Mars in 2012.

MARKS STUDENT MARGIN

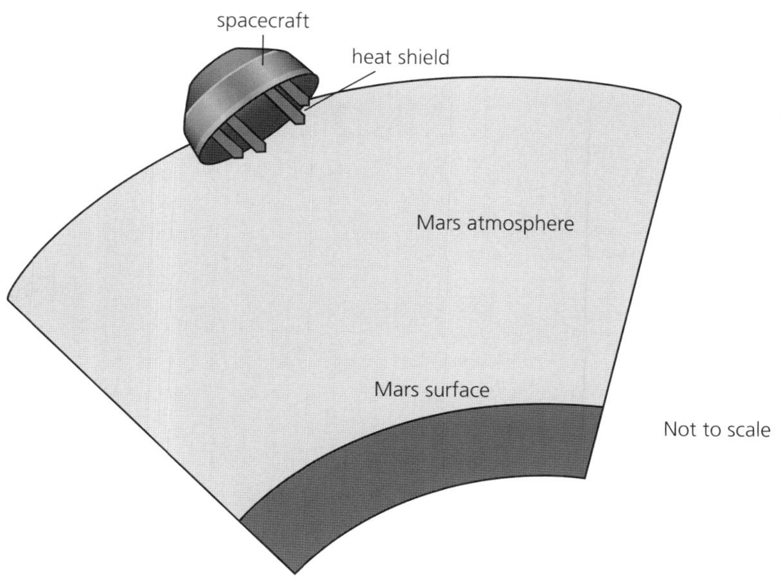

A spacecraft containing Curiosity entered the planet's atmosphere 125 km from its surface at a speed of $5900\ m\ s^{-1}$ and decelerated to a speed of around $400\ m\ s^{-1}$ at 11 km from the surface.

The average frictional force acting on the spacecraft was $3{\cdot}7 \times 10^5$ N.

a) **(i)** Calculate the work done by the frictional force on the spacecraft during this time. **3** CAS D&S4.3 HTP Page 99

Space for working and answer

11 a) (continued)

	MARKS	STUDENT MARGIN
(ii) Explain why a heat shield on the spacecraft was necessary for this part of the descent.	1	CAS D&S6.6 HTP Page 110
(iii) At 11 km from the surface, the spacecraft deployed a parachute to increase its deceleration. Explain why parachutes would have been ineffective to decelerate any spacecraft landing on the Moon.	1	CAS D&S4.1 HTP Page 108

11 (continued)

MARKS	STUDENT MARGIN

b) Closer to the surface of Mars, the spacecraft containing Curiosity shed its parachute, heatshield and outer shell.

The weight of the spacecraft at this stage was now 12 210 N.

(i) Show that the mass of the spacecraft at this stage was 3300 kg. **2** CAS D&S4.4 HTP Page 90

Space for working and answer

(ii) At 1·6 km from the surface, thruster engines were switched on to decelerate the spacecraft to a landing speed of around 1 m s^{-1}. The forces acting on the spacecraft at this time are shown in the diagram.

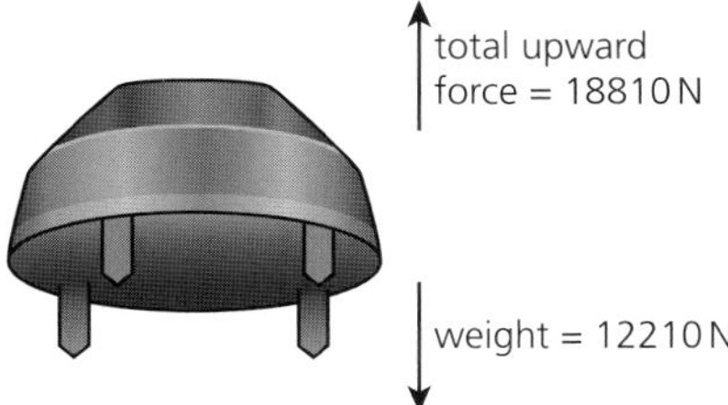

Calculate the magnitude of the deceleration of the spacecraft. **4** CAS D&S4.2 HTP Page 94

Space for working and answer

[END OF PRACTICE PAPER C]

Answers

National 5 Physics

Practice Paper A

SECTION 1

Question	Answer	Max mark	Hint
1	C	1	Calculate potential energy at heights 1·20 m and 0·95 m using $E_P = mgh$ and then calculate the difference. A quick method is to calculate the potential energy using the height difference of 0·25 m to obtain the answer directly.
2	B	1	Calculate the total amount of kinetic energy ($E_K = \frac{1}{2}mv^2$) at the starting speed of $10\,ms^{-1}$ since this is the maximum amount of energy that can be transformed into heat energy. Note that the time given in the question is not required in the calculation.
3	E	1	Charged particles experience a force when in an electric field. Direction of this force: Electrons towards the positive terminal, protons towards the negative terminal, neutrons have no charge and are unaffected. Hint – in questions like this, which offer choices of quantities X, Y and Z, it is sometimes helpful to mark the name of each particle on the diagram beside its path to make the correct selection of the answer easier.
4	D	1	The relationship to calculate charge is $Q = It$; note that the value of the resistor is not required in the calculation.
5	B	1	The battery potential difference is not given. There are two groups of resistors which are in series with each other. The same current is in each group. Current splits up in each group. The 10 Ω resistor is 3 times smaller than the 30 Ω resistor so it will have 3 times greater current. The 20 Ω resistor is half as much as the (35 + 5 =) 40 Ω resistance so it will have twice as much current. Consider how a current of 12 A splits up in the circuit. The greatest current is in the branch with the smallest resistance, i.e. 10 Ω. 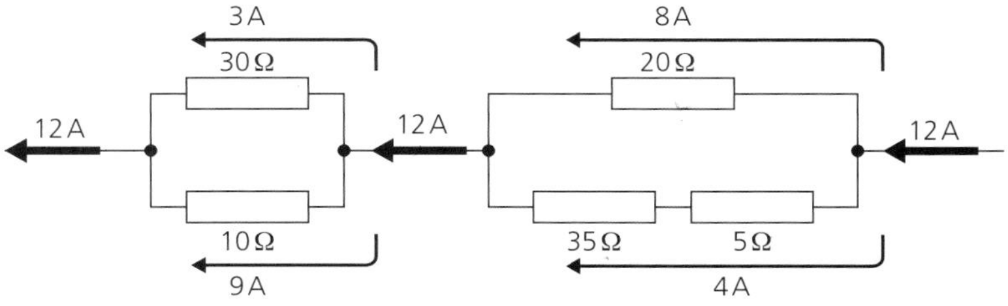 3 A 30 Ω; 10 Ω 9 A; 8 A 20 Ω; 35 Ω 5 Ω 4 A; 12 A; 12 A; 12 A
6	C	1	Calculate the pressure difference, Δp, between outside and inside pressure, then use this in $\Delta p = F/A$ to calculate the inward force.
7	B	1	Since pressure and kelvin temperature are directly proportional, a straight line graph through the origin is required.

Question	Answer	Max mark	Hint
8	C	1	wavespeed $v = \frac{\text{distance travelled}}{\text{time}} = \frac{85}{2{\cdot}5} = 34\,\text{ms}^{-1}$, wavelength $\lambda = \frac{85}{5\,\text{waves}} = 17$ m so frequency $f = \frac{v}{\lambda} = \frac{34}{17} = 2\,\text{Hz}$, amplitude $a = \frac{30}{2} = 15\,\text{m}$
9	E	1	Wavelength remains unchanged after diffraction of water waves, and the direction of the diffraction is always into the gap behind the barrier.
10	A	1	α particles consist of two protons and two neutrons, which is the configuration of a helium nucleus; β particles are electrons; both particles are emitted from atoms when they decay
11	D	1	Count rate is not reduced by paper, so α is not emitted by the source. Count rate is reduced (but not completely to background level) by aluminium which indicates that β is emitted by the source. Count rate is reduced, below the rate for aluminium, by lead, which indicates γ is emitted by the source.
12	A	1	To calculate E, use $D = \frac{E}{m}$; keep D in units of μGy and final answer for E will be in μJ.
13	E	1	Hint – in questions like this, which offer choices statements which are correct or incorrect, it is sometimes helpful to mark the correct statements with a tick to make the selection of the answer easier.
14	B	1	Hint – it is sometimes helpful to mark each quantity in the answers with 'v' for a vector and 's' for a scalar to make the selection of the answer easier.
15	A	1	The total distance is the sum of all the distances travelled in the journey; the displacement is the actual distance of the finish from the start position AND the direction of the finish from the start position.
16	D	1	The unbalanced force acting on the block is calculated using $F = ma = 5 \times 1{\cdot}2 = 6\,\text{N}$. This unbalanced force's direction must be to the left because the block is decelerating. The frictional force acts in the opposite direction to the direction of travel of the block. The frictional force is calculated by adding the unbalanced force of 6 N and the force pulling in the direction of movement, 54 N, to give 60 N. Unbalanced force = 6 N Frictional force = 54 + 6 = 60 N 5 kg 54 N
17	D	1	Force exerted by builder multiplied by distance travelled gives work done by builder, $E_W = Fd = 20 \times 120 = 2400\,\text{J}$

Question	Answer	Max mark	Hint
18	**C**	**1**	The unbalanced force acting on the module is calculated using $F = ma = 5000 \times 1{\cdot}4 = 7000\,\text{N}$. The weight of the module is calculated using $W = mg = 5000 \times 1{\cdot}6 = 8000\,\text{N}$. The module's engine must supply a thrust equal to the weight and the force causing the acceleration, Engine force $= 8000 + 7000 = 15\,000\,\text{N}$
19	**E**	**1**	The 'Newton pair' force is the reaction force to the aircraft engine exerting a force on the air, which is the air exerting a force on the aircraft engine.
20	**D**	**1**	Use $E = ml_f$ where l_f is obtained from the Data sheet in the table 'specific latent heat of fusion of materials'.

SECTION 2

Question			Answer	Max mark	Hint
1	a)		$I = \frac{1 \cdot 5}{3}$ $= 0 \cdot 5\,A$ (1)	1	Lamps are in parallel and identical, so each lamp has one third of the total current.
	b)		$P = IV$ (1) $= 0 \cdot 5 \times 4 \cdot 5$ (1) $= 2 \cdot 25\,W$ (1)	3	Lamps are connected in parallel so receive battery voltage. Use the value for current calculated in a).
	c)		The ammeter reading will increase. (1) Adding lamp in parallel reduces total resistance so current increases. (1)	2	When question requires a justification you must provide one (no justification means no marks will be awarded, even if your first statement is correct!)
				(6)	
2	a)	(i)	$V_R = V_{supply} - V_{LDR} = 3 \cdot 0\,V$ (1) $V_R = IR$ (1) $3 \cdot 0 = I \times 2250$ $I = 1 \cdot 333 \times 10^{-3}\,A$ $V_{LDR} = IR_{LDR}$ (1) $2 \cdot 0 = 1 \cdot 333 \times 10^{-3} \times R_{LDR}$ $R_{LDR} = 1500\,\Omega$ (1)	4	The voltage across the variable resistor (V_R) has to be calculated first by subtracting the voltage across the LDR (V_{LDR}) from the battery voltage (V_{supply}). Use the voltage across the variable resistor and its resistance to calculate the current in the circuit using Ohm's Law. Use the current in the LDR and the voltage across it to calculate its resistance, again using Ohm's Law.
		(ii)	140 units	1	Use the value calculated in a) (i) for the LDR resistance. Use a ruler along the graph to obtain an accurate reading.
	b)	(i)	As R_{LDR} increases, V_{LDR} increases. (1) When V_{LDR} reaches switching voltage, the MOSFET turns on. (1) Current is now in the relay which completes the lamp circuit. (1)	3	Explain questions usually require one important fact per mark available in the question. Here, the important things to mention are: what happens to the voltage across the LDR as the light level increases, what happens to the MOSFET when this voltage increases, what happens to the relay when the MOSFET switches on.

Question			Answer	Max mark	Hint
		(ii)	Lamps will switch on at a lower outside light level. Resistance of LDR must be greater than 1500 Ω (1) to maintain the MOSFET switching voltage. (1)	3	In this type of question, you must state whether the new outside light level which the lamps switch on at would be higher, lower or unchanged. In this case, the lamps will switch on at a lower light level. The justification should explain that if the variable resistor's resistance is increased, then a lower light level would be required to cause an increase in the LDR resistance. This would cause the voltage across the LDR to reach the voltage required to switch on the MOSFET.
				(11)	
3	a)		$E_h = cm\Delta T$ (1) $= 1800 \times 2{\cdot}8 \times 150$ (1) $E_h = 756\,000$ J (1)	3	Temperature change, $\Delta T = 170 - 20 = 150$ °C, must be calculated first. Then use $E_h = cm\,\Delta T$ to calculate the energy required.
	b)		$P = \frac{E_h}{t}$ (1) $1500 = \frac{756\,000}{t}$ (1) $t = 504$ s (1)	3	Use the energy calculated in a), and use the power rating given in the rating plate in the diagram for the appliance. Calculate time, t, using $P = \frac{E_h}{t}$.
	c)	(i)	Heat energy loss from the appliance to the surroundings means it will take longer to supply the energy required to heat the oil to 170 °C. (1)	1	When determining the time to heat a substance, energy loss to the surroundings is always a factor which extends the time required.
		(ii)	Use a cover/lid etc. (1)	1	A cover increases the insulation around the appliance and reduces the heat loss.
				(8)	
4	a)		$T_1 = 20\,°C = 293$ K $T_2 = 28\,°C = 301$ K $\frac{p_1}{T_1} = \frac{p_2}{T_2}$ (1) $\frac{100}{293} = \frac{p_2}{301}$ (1) $p_2 = 103$ kPa (1)	3	Temperature must be converted from °C into kelvins by adding 273. Use $\frac{p_1}{T_1} = \frac{p_2}{T_2}$ to calculate p_2. Note that p_1 can be used in the equations in kPa units, producing an answer for p_2 in kPa units.
	b)		As temperature increases, the average E_k of the gas particles increases, (1) so the particles collide with the walls of the container more frequently with greater force (1) so pressure increases. (1)	3	The three marks available indicate that three separate points should be mentioned. When answering the question, try to present the information in logical steps starting with the effect of increasing temperature (increasing temperature means average E_k of gas particles increases).

Question			Answer	Max mark	Hint
	c)		Place temperature sensor inside the flask to measure gas temperature directly.	1	This allows the exact temperature of the gas to be measured when the pressure reading of the gas is made.
				(7)	
5	a)		$T = \frac{1}{f}$ (1) $4{\cdot}0 \times 10^{10} = \frac{1}{f}$ (1) $f = 2{\cdot}5 \times 10^{9}$ Hz (1)	3	There is no requirement to convert the frequency into MHz or GHz in the final answer.
	b)		$v = f\lambda$ (1) $3 \times 10^{8} = 2{\cdot}5 \times 10^{9} \times \lambda$ (1) $\lambda = 0{\cdot}12$ m (1)	3	Use the value for frequency calculated in a). All waves in the electromagnetic spectrum, including microwaves, travel at the speed of light in vacuum. This value is found in the Data sheet.
				(6)	

Question			Answer	Max mark	Hint
6			**Sample answer** Astronomical objects in space, like stars and galaxies, emit electromagnetic radiation across all bands of the electromagnetic spectrum. The higher the frequency of the electromagnetic radiation bands, the greater the energy of the radiation emitted. Different detectors are required to receive signals from these different bands. Telescopes contain different detectors to receive the signals of each particular band in the electromagnetic spectrum. Gamma rays, X-rays, UV and infrared rays from space are absorbed by the Earth's atmosphere. To detect these signals, telescopes must be carried on satellites above the Earth's atmosphere. Optical telescopes are used to detect visible light and can be Earth based. Light from stars and galaxies can be analysed to obtain line spectra which can identify the elements present. Infrared telescopes can be used to detect infrared radiation from stars and galaxies which are obscured behind dense regions of dust or gas which do not allow visible light to pass through. Radio telescopes detect radio waves which can be used to help produce maps of the positions of astronomical objects in space.	3	This is an open-ended question: a variety of physics arguments can be used to answer this question. Marks are awarded on the basis of whether the answer overall demonstrates 'no', 'limited', 'reasonable' or 'good' understanding. Demonstrates no understanding: 0 marks Demonstrates limited understanding: 1 mark Demonstrates reasonable understanding: 2 marks Demonstrates good understanding: 3 marks Three marks would be awarded to an answer which demonstrates a good understanding of the physics involved. The answer would show a good comprehension of the physics of the situation, provided in a logically correct sequence. (This type of answer might include a statement of the principles involved, a relationship or an equation, and the application of these to respond to the problem.) This does not mean the answer has to be what might be termed an 'excellent' answer or a 'complete' one. Also, note that the open-ended type of question is worth three marks. It is important not to spend too much time answering this question (3–4 minutes is the average time in the paper for 3 marks). A guide would be to take perhaps 3–5 minutes to complete this type of question. Only use more time than this if you have completed and checked all of the remaining questions in the paper.
				(3)	

Question			Answer	Max mark	Hint
7	a)	(i)	Refraction occurs when light travels from one medium into another with a change in the wave speed and wavelength.	1	Both speed and wavelength of light decrease when it passes into an 'optically denser' material e.g. from air into glass. Note that during refraction, the frequency of the light remains constant.
		(ii)	1 mark for showing refraction towards normal in glass. 1 mark for showing refraction away from normal when emerging from glass into air.	2	It is always best to use a ruler to complete straight lines on diagrams. The refracted light ray entering the glass always changes direction towards the normal, and returns to the original direction when it emerges into the air again.
		(iii)	1 mark for correct identification of one angle of incidence. 	1	The angle of incidence is the angle between the ray and the normal as it approaches a boundary (in this case either: air into glass, or emerging from glass into air).
	b)	(i)	X: infrared (1) Y: ultraviolet (1)	2	The order of the bands of the electromagnetic spectrum should be memorised along with the order of increasing wavelength or frequency of these bands.
		(ii)	$v = \frac{d}{t}$ (1) $3 \times 10^8 = \frac{6{\cdot}7 \times 10^{11}}{t}$ (1) $t = 2{\cdot}2 \times 10^3$ s (1)	3	Remember, all waves in the electromagnetic spectrum, including microwaves, travel at the speed of light, 3×10^8 ms^{-1} in a vacuum (or air). This value is found in the Data sheet. It is not necessary to convert time into minutes.
				(9)	
8	a)	(i)	Half-life is the time for the activity of a radioactive substance to reduce to half of its original value.	1	The definition of half-life is a standard question and should be memorised.
		(ii)	12 hours	1	It is convenient to start with 80 kBq which is at time zero, then find the time on the graph for half (40 kBq); this allows the time to be read directly (12 hours). Care is needed when using the time scale (in this case 2 hours per division).
		(iii)	$80 \rightarrow 40 \rightarrow 20 \rightarrow 10$ (1) 10 kBq (1)	2	Use the value for half-life calculated in a) (ii). From the starting activity (80 kBq), halve this value three times; always state the final answer (including unit kBq).

Question			Answer	Max mark	Hint
	b)	(i)	$H = Dw_r$ (1) $= 15 \times 2$ (1) $= 30\ \mu Sv$ (1)	3	The radiation weighting factor, w_r, is given in this question. Note that the given unit for absorbed dose, D, in μGy can be used directly without changing back to Gy. This means that the calculated value for equivalent dose, H, would be in units of μSv.
		(ii)	$\dot{H} = \frac{H}{t}$ (1) $= \frac{30}{3}$ (1) $= 10\ \mu Svh^{-1}$ (1)	3	When writing the relationship, $\dot{H} = \frac{H}{t}$, it is important to correctly represent equivalent dose rate, $\dot{H}$, with a clearly marked dot above. Use time, t, in the same units as given in the question (hours).
				(10)	
9	a)		$W = mg$ (1) $= 9{\cdot}7 \times 10^7 \times 9{\cdot}8$ (1) $= 9{\cdot}5 \times 10^8$ N (1)	3	Remember to state the correct units for weight, newtons, N.
	b)		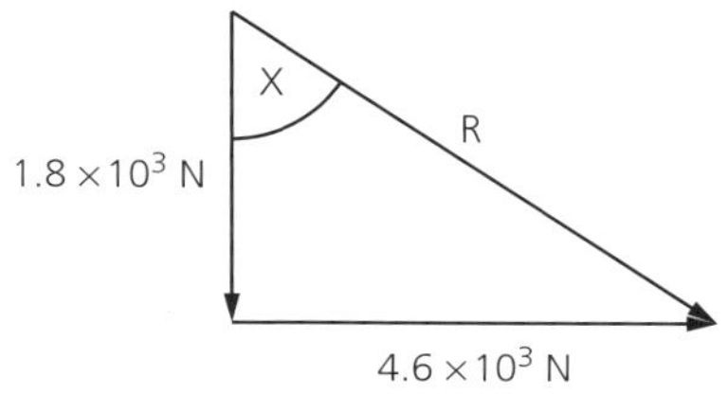 $R^2 = (1{\cdot}8 \times 10^3)^2 + (4{\cdot}6 \times 10^3)^2$ (1) $R = 4{\cdot}9 \times 10^3$ N (1) $\tan x = \frac{4{\cdot}6 \times 10^3}{1{\cdot}8 \times 10^3}$ (1) $x = 69°$ Resultant force = $4{\cdot}9 \times 10^3$ N at bearing of 111° (1)	4	The answer can be obtained by drawing a scale diagram, marks are awarded thus: 1 mark for drawing a diagram to a reasonable scale, and for lines drawn with correct length and angle 1 mark for adding the engine force and tide vectors correctly showing resultant direction (arrow needed) 1 mark for force $F = 4{\cdot}9 \times 10^3$ N 1 mark for bearing of 111°, (or 21° South of East).
				(7)	
10	a)	(i)	$a = \frac{v - u}{t}$ (1) $= \frac{0 - 16}{30}$ (1) $= -0{\cdot}53\ m\,s^{-2}$ (1)	3	Care is required to select the correct values for u (16 ms^{-1}) and v (0 ms^{-1}) from the graph, and to use them correctly in $a = \frac{(v-u)}{t}$. The negative answer means that the cyclist is decelerating.
		(ii)	Cyclist is moving at constant speed.	1	C to D is horizontal, meaning constant speed on a speed–time graph.

n			Answer	Max mark	Hint
		(iii)	forward force → ← friction	2	Since the cyclist moves at constant speed between C and D, the forces acting on the cyclist are balanced. The forward force is balanced by frictional force. 1 mark for showing the direction arrow and name of the forward force, 1 mark for showing the direction arrow and name of the frictional force.
	b)	(i)	Total distance = area under speed / time graph (1) $= \frac{1}{2} \times 25 \times 16 + 195 \times 16 + \frac{1}{2} \times 30 \times 16$ (1) $= 3560\,\text{m}$ (1)	3	Take care to identify every shape (triangles and rectangles). Then carefully extract the values from the graph for each shape.
		(ii)	$\bar{v} = \frac{d}{t}$ (1) $= \frac{3560}{250}$ (1) $= 14{\cdot}24\,\text{m s}^{-1}$ (1)	3	Use the value for distance calculated in b)(i).
				(12)	
11	a)		$a = \frac{v-u}{t}$ (1) $9{\cdot}8 = \frac{v-0}{0{\cdot}55}$ (1) $v = 5{\cdot}39\,\text{m s}^{-1}$ (1)	3	The ball accelerates vertically downwards at $9{\cdot}8\,\text{m s}^{-2}$ for 0·55 seconds.
	b)		$\bar{v} = \frac{u+v}{2} = \frac{0+5{\cdot}39}{2} = 2{\cdot}7\,\text{m s}^{-1}$ (1) $d = \bar{v}t$ (1) $2{\cdot}7 = \frac{d}{0{\cdot}55}$ (1) $d = 1{\cdot}49\,\text{m}$ (1)	4	Work out average vertical speed, using value for final vertical speed calculated in a). Then use average velocity relationship $d = \bar{v}t$ to calculate the vertical height of position X.
	c)		Time for ball to fall to ground is the same as in part a).	1	The ball falls for the same vertical height in both demonstrations, so the time in the air is the same.
				(8)	

Question			Answer	Max mark	Hint
12			**Sample answer** Spacecraft have to be able to travel at high speeds to travel large distances in a reasonable time. Rocket engines use a huge amount of conventional fuel at launch simply to get a spacecraft into space. The spacecraft itself has a limited capacity for conventional fuel. An ion drive engine produces a beam of gas ions which are expelled with a force from the engine nozzle; there is a reaction force on the nozzle which causes acceleration of the spacecraft. This force is typically very small which means that the acceleration is very small. The ion drive engine must operate for a long time before the spacecraft reaches its top speed. Electrical energy required to operate the ion drive is obtained from a solar panel array or a nuclear generator. Gravity assist allows a spacecraft to increase its speed by 'flying by' a planet. As the spacecraft approaches the planet, a gravitational attractive force causes the spacecraft to start orbiting the planet which is moving in orbit around the sun. When the spacecraft leaves this planetary orbit some of the kinetic energy of the moving planet is transferred to it, and its speed increases.	(3)	This is an open-ended question: a variety of physics arguments can be used to answer this question. Marks are awarded on the basis of whether the answer overall demonstrates 'no', 'limited', 'reasonable' or 'good' understanding. Demonstrates no understanding: 0 marks Demonstrates limited understanding: 1 mark Demonstrates reasonable understanding: 2 marks Demonstrates good understanding: 3 marks Three marks would be awarded to an answer which demonstrates a good understanding of the physics involved. The answer would show a good comprehension of the physics of the situation, provided in a logically correct sequence. (This type of answer might include a statement of the principles involved, a relationship or an equation, and the application of these to respond to the problem.) This does not mean the answer has to be what might be termed an 'excellent' answer or a 'complete' one. Also, note that the open-ended type of question is worth three marks. It is important not to spend too much time answering this question (3–4 minutes is the average time in the paper for 3 marks). A guide would be to take perhaps 3–5 minutes to complete this type of question. Only use more time than this if you have completed and checked all of the remaining questions in the paper.

Practice Paper B

SECTION 1

Question	Answer	Max mark	Hint
1	A	1	The loss of potential energy is calculated using $E_p = mgh$ where $h = 0{\cdot}5$ m and $g = 9{\cdot}8\,\text{N kg}^{-1}$. Note that the length of the track and the frictional force are not required in this calculation.
2	D	1	First, calculate the current in the device with $P = IV$, using $V = 230$ V and $P = 9200$ W (from rating plate), then use $Q = It$, converting 5 minutes into seconds.
3	B	1	Use $V = IR$ where $V = 6$ V and $I = 0{\cdot}5$ A to calculate total resistance in the circuit, then subtract $5\,\Omega$ from the total resistance to obtain resistance of R.
4	D	1	Use $\frac{1}{R_T} = \frac{1}{R_1} + \frac{1}{R_2} + \frac{1}{R_3}$ to determine the resistance of resistors in parallel, and then add this answer to the $4\,\Omega$ resistor in series to get total resistance.
5	C	1	The temperature of the air inside the syringe remains constant. This means that the average speed of the molecules does not change, and also that the air molecules do not strike the walls inside the syringe with greater force. However, because of the reduced volume, the air molecules collide with the walls inside the syringe more often.
6	B	1	Temperature change, $\Delta T = 70 - -15 = 85$ °C, is the same in kelvins as it is in °C.
7	D	1	Since $f = \frac{v}{\lambda}$, the smallest wavelength will produce the highest frequency. $f = \frac{v}{\lambda} = \frac{340}{0{\cdot}04} = 8500\,\text{Hz} = 8{\cdot}5\,\text{kHz}$
8	E	1	When moving from air into another medium, the speed and wavelength of light always change.
9	A	1	When light travels from glass into air or air to glass, the angle between the normal and the light ray is always greater in air than in glass.
10	E	1	Use $A = \frac{N}{t}$ to calculate N; convert kBq into Bq and minutes into seconds.
11	E	1	Alpha radiation causes high ionisation of air and has a long half-life of 432 years.
12	B	1	Use $\dot{H} = \frac{H}{t}$; change $0{\cdot}08\,\mu\text{Sv}$ into $8{\cdot}0 \times 10^{-8}$; keep time in hours.

Question	Answer	Max mark	Hint
13	D	1	The net horizontal force is 10 kN to the East and the net vertical force is 10 kN South, so the resultant force must be in the direction between East and South.
14	E	1	Displacement = area under velocity-time graph $= \frac{1}{2} \times 2{\cdot}5 \times -8 + \frac{1}{2} \times 2{\cdot}5 \times -8$ $= -10 + 10 = 0$ m $= -10 + 10 = 0$ m Acceleration $= \dfrac{v-u}{t} = \dfrac{8--8}{5} = 3{\cdot}2\,\text{ms}^{-2}$
15	B	1	$F_{un} = 4 - 2 = 2$N to the left, $a = \dfrac{F}{m} = \dfrac{-2}{4} = -0{\cdot}5\,\text{ms}^{-2}$, after 2 seconds, final velocity $v = u + at$ $= 4 + (-0{\cdot}5 \times 2) = 3\,\text{ms}^{-1}$
16	C	1	At 400 km, $g = 8{\cdot}6$ ms^{-2}, $W = mg = 90 \times 8{\cdot}6 = 774$ N
17	A	1	Weight of module on Moon $W = mg = 5000 \times 1{\cdot}6 = 8000$ N, $F_{un} = 15\,000 -$ weight $= 15\,000 - 8000 = 7000$ N, $a = \dfrac{F}{m} = \dfrac{-7000}{5000}$ $= 1{\cdot}4\,\text{ms}^{-2}$
18	A	1	Rocket engines exert a downward force on exhaust gases so the reaction force is exhaust gases exerting an upward force on the rocket engines.
19	D	1	Each ball takes the same time to reach the floor, because they are released from the same height. Different horizontal distances travelled mean that the horizontal velocities are different. Both balls fall for the same time from rest, so have the same final vertical velocities.
20	B	1	number of light years $= \dfrac{\text{total distance travelled by light from star}}{\text{distance travelled by light in one year}}$ $= \dfrac{4{\cdot}2 \times 10^{16}}{3 \times 10^{8} \times 365 \times 24 \times 60 \times 60} = 4{\cdot}4$ Note that 365·25 days (the average number of days in one year) also gives the same result of 4·4.

B

SECTION 2

Question			Answer	Max mark	Hint
1	a)		Negative	1	Particle must have negative charge because it experiences an upward force due to the electric field towards the positive metal plate.
	b)		$W = mg$ (1) $= 5{\cdot}4 \times 10^{-8} \times 9{\cdot}8$ (1) $= 5{\cdot}3 \times 10^{-7}\,\text{N}$ (1)	3	Remember to state the correct units for weight, newtons, N.
	c)		Particle moves at constant velocity. (1) Forces are now balanced. (1)	2	After 3 seconds, the horizontal line on the graph means constant velocity, so the forces on the particle are balanced.
				(6)	
2	a)		Adjust variable resistor	1	This alters total resistance in the circuit, altering the current in the circuit.
	b)	(i)	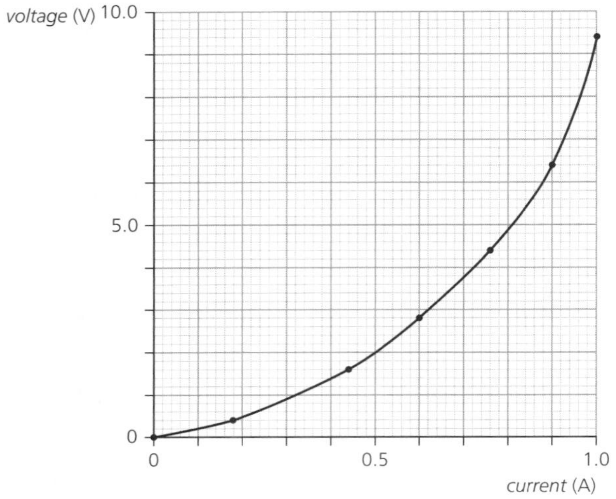 voltage (V) 10.0, 5.0, 0; current (A) 0, 0.5, 1.0 Suitable scales, labels and units (1) All points plotted accurately to ± half a division (1) Best-fit curve (1)	3	Take care to choose suitable scales which will produce a graph of reasonable size on the grid provided (remember that a spare grid is always provided at the end of the question paper if you need to redraw your graph). The labels for each axis should be clearly identified with the correct unit supplied. The points must be plotted accurately. The final curve should be 'best fit' i.e. smoothly drawn through as many points as possible (but never simply join the plotted points to produce a 'zig-zag' effect).
		(ii)	1·2 V	1	Use a ruler along the graph to obtain an accurate reading.
		(iii)	Resistance increases as current increases (1) When $I = 0{\cdot}44\,\text{A}$, $V = 1{\cdot}6\,\text{V}$, so $R = \frac{V}{I} = 3{\cdot}6\,\Omega$ (1) When $I = 1{\cdot}0\,\text{A}$, $V = 9{\cdot}6\,\text{V}$, so $R = \frac{V}{I} = 9{\cdot}6\,\Omega$ (1)	3	An explanation is required, so choose values for voltage and current at different parts of the graph to calculate and show the lamp's resistance at these points.
				(8)	

Question			Answer		Max mark	Hint
3	a)	(i)	Lamps must operate at 230 V. In parallel, each lamp receives the supply voltage (230 V).	(1)	1	For each lamp to receive 230 V, they must be connected in parallel with the supply.
		(ii)	$P=\frac{V^2}{R}$ $50=\frac{230^2}{R}$ $R=1058\,\Omega$	(1) (1) (1)	3	Select the relationship $P=\frac{V^2}{R}$ to calculate the lamp resistance because the power and operating voltage of the lamp are given.
	b)		Total power $=3\times 50=150$ W $P=IV$ $150=I\times 230$ $I=0{\cdot}65$ A	(1) (1) (1)	3	To calculate total current, use the total power of all 3 lamps.
					(7)	
4	a)		$E_h=cm\Delta T$ $=4180\times 0{\cdot}6\times 75$ $E_h=188\,100$ J	(1) (1) (1)	3	Temperature change, $\Delta T = 100 - 25 = 75$ °C, must be calculated first. Then use $E_H = cm\,\Delta T$ to calculate the energy required.
	b)	(i)	$P=\frac{E}{t}$ $800=\frac{E}{12\times 60}$ $E=576\,000$ J	(1) (1) (1)	3	Remember, time must be converted into seconds for this relationship.
		(ii)	$E_h=ml_v$ $576\,000=m\times 22{\cdot}6\times 10^5$ $m=0{\cdot}25$ kg	(1) (1) (1)	3	Use the energy calculated in b) (ii) in this relationship. The value for the specific latent heat of vaporisation, l_v, is found in the Data sheet.
		(iii)	Some of the heat energy supplied will be lost to the surroundings and so less will be available to convert water into steam.		1	There is always energy lost to the surroundings whenever a substance is heated by an appliance. This heat energy loss from the steamer to the surroundings means that there will be less energy available to convert water into steam.
					(10)	

Question			Answer	Max mark	Hint
5	a)		$T_1 = 10\,°C = 283\,K$, $T_2 = -40\,°C = 233\,K$, $p_1 = 1{\cdot}01 \times 10^5$ $\frac{p_1}{T_1} = \frac{p_2}{T_2}$ (1) $\frac{1{\cdot}01 \times 10^5}{283} = \frac{p_2}{233}$ (1) $p_2 = 8{\cdot}3 \times 10^4\,Pa$ (1)	3	Temperature must be converted from °C into kelvins by adding 273. Use $\frac{p_1}{T_1} = \frac{p_2}{T_2}$, to calculate p_2
	b)	(i)	$\Delta p = 1{\cdot}01 \times 10^5 - 8{\cdot}3 \times 10^4$ $= 1{\cdot}8 \times 10^4\ Pa$	1	Use the answer to a) in this calculation.
		(ii)	$P = \frac{F}{A}$ (1) $1{\cdot}8 \times 10^4 = \frac{F}{0{\cdot}45}$ (1) $F = 8100\,N$ (1)	3	The air pressure difference between inside and outside the container, calculated in b) (i), is used in this relationship.
		(iii)	Downwards on lid	1	The air pressure outside the container is greater than the pressure inside, so the resulting pressure is downwards on the lid.
				(8)	
6			**Sample answer** There is more diffraction of sound than of light; sound waves have longer wavelength than light waves, so the sounds of the dog are likely to diffract towards the student around fences or trees. Light waves are less likely to diffract enough to illuminate the side of the field, and the light from the torch is directed into a narrow beam. The sounds of the dog may reflect off fences or trees to reach the student.		This is an open-ended question: a variety of physics arguments can be used to answer this question. Marks are awarded on the basis of whether the answer overall demonstrates 'no', 'limited', 'reasonable' or 'good' understanding.

Question			Answer	Max mark	Hint
			Sound waves are more likely to travel in all directions from the dog, allowing the student to hear the sounds directly without requiring diffraction.	3	Demonstrates no understanding: 0 marks Demonstrates limited understanding: 1 mark Demonstrates reasonable understanding: 2 marks Demonstrates good understanding: 3 marks Three marks would be awarded to an answer which demonstrates a good understanding of the physics involved. The answer would show a good comprehension of the physics of the situation, provided in a logically correct sequence. (This type of answer might include a statement of the principles involved, a relationship or an equation, and the application of these to respond to the problem.) This does not mean the answer has to be what might be termed an 'excellent' answer or a 'complete' one. Also, note that the open-ended type of question is worth three marks. It is important not to spend too much time answering this question (3–4 minutes is the average time in the paper for 3 marks). A guide would be to take perhaps 3–5 minutes to complete this type of question. Only use more time than this if you have completed and checked all of the remaining questions in the paper.
				(3)	
7	**a)**		The direction of current from an alternating supply changes at the frequency of the supply. The current from a direct supply always moves in the same direction.	1	It is essential to clearly describe each type of current to identify the difference between them.

Question			Answer	Max mark	Hint
	b)	(i)	Amplitude $= 3 \times 2{\cdot}5 = 7{\cdot}5\,\text{V}$	1	There are 3 centimetres from the centre to the top of the waveform, and the volts per centimetre setting is 2·5 volts.
		(ii)	Time T for 1 wave: $8 \times 0{\cdot}4 \times 10^{-3} = 3{\cdot}2 \times 10^{-3}\,\text{s}$	1	One complete wave occupies 8 boxes on the horizontal axis. The timescale setting is 0·4 milliseconds per centimetre, so total time for the wave (the period, T) is number of centimetres × timescale setting.
		(iii)	$T = \frac{1}{f}$ (1) $3{\cdot}2 \times 10^{-3} = \frac{1}{f}$ (1) $f = 312{\cdot}5\,\text{Hz}$ (1)	3	Use the value for T calculated in b) (ii).
	c)	(i)	W only	1	d.c. circuit: In circuit A, the LED conducts current from the negative terminal to the positive terminal in W only. The orientation of LEDs Y and Z are the wrong way for conduction and so prevent current in the remaining branches.
		(ii)	W and Z	1	a.c. circuit: In an alternating current circuit, W and Z will conduct for each separate direction of the alternating current, but X and Y connected together in series will prevent any conduction of current in them.
				(8)	
8	a)	(i)	1. Chandra 2. IRIS 3. WISE	2	The order of the bands of the electromagnetic spectrum should be memorised, and the order of increasing wavelength or frequency of these bands. (2 marks for all correctly identified; 1 mark for 1 correctly identified.)

Question			Answer	Max mark	Hint
		(ii)	1. WISE 2. IRIS 3. Chandra	2	Remember, the relationship between the altitude of a satellite and its period is: the greater the altitude, the greater the period of the satellite. (2 marks for all correctly identified; 1 mark for 1 correctly identified.)
	b)		$v = f\lambda$ (1) $3\times10^{8} = f\times2{\cdot}5\times10^{-7}$ (1) $f = 1{\cdot}2\times10^{15}\,\text{Hz}$ (1)	3	Remember, all waves in the electromagnetic spectrum, including ultraviolet waves, travel at the speed of light, 3×10^{8} ms^{-1} in a vacuum (or air). This value is found in the Data sheet.
	c)		$d = vt$ (1) $105\,000 \times 10^{3} = 3 \times 10^{8} \times t$ (1) $t = 0{\cdot}35\,\text{s}$ (1)	3	Use the altitude given in the table for the distance travelled by the radio signal. Remember, radio signals travel at the speed of light, 3×10^{8} ms^{-1} in a vacuum (or air).
	d)		Radiation from some bands of the electromagnetic spectrum is absorbed by the Earth's atmosphere, so some telescopes need to be above the atmosphere to detect this radiation.	1	It is not necessary, in this answer, to name the bands of radiation which are absorbed by the Earth's atmosphere.
				(11)	
9	a)		Neutron	1	A qualitative description of nuclear fission (and fusion) is required in N5.
	b)	(i)	$1000 \rightarrow 500$ (From graph: $0 \rightarrow 200$ years) so half-life is 200 years	1	It is convenient with this graph to start with 1000 kBq which is at the start of the time axis, then find the time on the graph for half (500 kBq) which is at 200 years. This allows the half-life to be easily assessed from the graph.

Question			Answer	Max mark	Hint
		(ii)	$1000 \rightarrow 500 \rightarrow 250 \rightarrow 125 \rightarrow 62{\cdot}5$ is 4 half-lives (1) So total time $= 4 \times 200 = 800$ years (1)	2	Use the half-life calculated in b). From the starting activity (1000 kBq) halve this value until 62.5 kBq is reached. Always state the final answer (including the unit, years).
	c)	(i)	$D = \frac{E}{m}$ (1) $= \frac{850 \times 10^{-6}}{70}$ (1) $= 1{\cdot}2 \times 10^{-5}$ Gy (1)	3	The relationship $D = \frac{E}{m}$ does not require the nature of the ionising radiation to be taken into account. Only the energy absorbed and the mass of the absorbing tissue are required.
		(ii)	$H = Dw_r$ (1) $= 1{\cdot}2 \times 10^{-5} \times 20$ (1) $= 2{\cdot}4 \times 10^{-4}$ Sv (1)	3	Use the value for the absorbed dose, D, from c) (i). The relationship $H = Dw_r$ to determine the equivalent dose requires the radiation weighting factor for the ionising radiation, w_r, to be obtained from the table of radiation weighting factors in the Data sheet (in this case, $w_r = 20$ for alpha radiation). If the type of ionising radiation is not in this table, then the value for w_r will appear in the question.
		(iii)	Worker should wear protective clothing	1	This precaution is one safety measure when dealing with radiation.
	d)		Nuclear fusion	1	The question is mainly about nuclear fission. Nuclear fusion is the other nuclear process involved in the generation of electricity.
				(12)	
10	a)	(i)	50 N	1	Care is required when identifying the correct point for the force on the graph corresponding to 0·35 m.
		(ii)	$E_w = Fd$ (1) $= 50 \times 0{\cdot}35$ (1) $E_w = 17{\cdot}5$ J (1)	3	Use the answer determined in a) (i) for the distance, d.

Question			Answer	Max mark	Hint
	b)	(i)	$s = \bar{v}t$ (1) $30 = 40 \times t$ (1) $t = 0{\cdot}75\,s$ (1)	3	The horizontal velocity, $\bar{v}$, is constant because air resistance is ignored.
		(ii)	$E_K = \frac{1}{2}mv^2$ (1) $= \frac{1}{2} \times 0{\cdot}06 \times 40^2$ (1) $E_K = 48\,J$ (1)	3	Take care when using $E_K = \frac{1}{2}mv^2$ to square the value of the speed when calculating the answer.
		(iii)	40 m s⁻¹ / X / V / 7.35 m s⁻¹ / Horizontal direction $v^2 = 40^2 + 7{\cdot}35^2$ (1) $v = 40{\cdot}1\,m\,s^{-1}$ (1) $\tan x = \frac{7.35}{40}$ (1) $x = 10{\cdot}4°$ Resultant velocity is $40{\cdot}1\,m\,s^{-1}$ at $10{\cdot}4°$ below horizontal. (1)	4	The answer can be obtained by drawing a scale diagram; marks are awarded thus: 1 mark for drawing a diagram to a reasonable scale, and for lines drawn with correct length and angle 1 mark for adding the horizontal velocity and final vertical velocity vectors and correctly showing resultant direction (arrow needed) 1 mark for resultant $v = 40{\cdot}1\,ms^{-1}$ 1 mark for direction of $10{\cdot}4°$ below horizontal
				(14)	

Question			Answer	Max mark	Hint
11			**Sample answer** On the motorway, driving tends to be for long journeys at higher constant speeds than in town. This means that the engine uses energy only to overcome frictional forces. In town driving, there are many occasions where the car must slow down and then accelerate. In addition to the energy required to maintain constant speed, additional energy to produce the unbalanced force required for acceleration is needed. On the occasions when cars are in long queues or traffic jams, energy is used up while the car engine idles. This is possible on motorways and in towns. The car design also affects how much energy the car uses; if the car is streamlined, then less fuel will be required to overcome air friction.	3	This is an open-ended question: a variety of physics arguments can be used to answer this question. Marks are awarded on the basis of whether the answer overall demonstrates 'no', 'limited', 'reasonable' or 'good' understanding. Demonstrates no understanding: 0 marks Demonstrates limited understanding: 1 mark Demonstrates reasonable understanding: 2 marks Demonstrates good understanding: 3 marks Three marks would be awarded to an answer which demonstrates a good understanding of the physics involved. The answer would show a good comprehension of the physics of the situation, provided in a logically correct sequence. (This type of answer might include a statement of the principles involved, a relationship or an equation, and the application of these to respond to the problem.) This does not mean the answer has to be what might be termed an 'excellent' answer or a 'complete' one. Also, note that the open-ended type of question is worth three marks. It is important not to spend too much time answering this question (3–4 minutes is the average time in the paper for 3 marks). A guide would be to take perhaps 3–5 minutes to complete this type of question. Only use more time than this if you have completed and checked all of the remaining questions in the paper.
				(3)	

Practice Paper C

SECTION 1

Question	Answer	Max mark	Hint
1	D	1	First calculate the current using Ohm's Law: $I = \frac{V_s}{\text{total resistance}} = \frac{60}{30} = 2A$. The charge passing through the series circuit has the same value at all positions. The relationship used to calculate charge is Q = It, (convert 2 minutes into seconds).
2	B	1	Use Ohm's Law, $V = IR$, to calculate each resistor using values for V and I from the graph. $V = IR_P$ $20 = 2 \times R_P$, $R_P = 10\,\Omega$ $V = IR_Q$, $10 = 4 \times R_Q$, $R_Q = 2.5\,\Omega$
3	C	1	First, calculate the total resistance of each of the two branches which have resistors connected in series: $R_T = R_1 + R_2 = 12 + 12 = 24\,\Omega$ Then calculate the total resistance of the three branches of resistors connected in parallel: $\frac{1}{R_T} = \frac{1}{R_1} + \frac{1}{R_2} + \frac{1}{R_3} = \frac{1}{24} + \frac{1}{6} + \frac{1}{24} = 0.25$, $R_r = \frac{1}{0.25} = 4\Omega$
4	E	1	When the variable resistor's resistance is decreased, the share of the battery voltage across the variable resistor (voltmeter V_1) decreases, and the share of the battery voltage across the fixed resistor (voltmeter V_2) increases. Also, the total resistance in the circuit decreases. This means that the current (and ammeter reading) increases.
5	B	1	The circuit symbol, function and application of standard electrical and electronic components should be studied and memorised. LDR: [symbol]
6	A	1	To calculate R, use $P = I^2R$, $48 = 2^2 \times R$, $R = 12\,\Omega$ To calculate V, use $P = IV$, $48 = 2 \times V$, $V = 24$ V
7	B	1	The volume of a fixed mass of gas at constant temperature is inversely proportional to its pressure, so a graph of pressure p against $\frac{1}{V}$ will produce a straight line graph through the origin.
8	D	1	When light travels from air into glass: its speed decreases its frequency stays constant its wavelength decreases.

Question	Answer	Max mark	Hint
9	E	1	Both alpha and beta radiation are absorbed by 5 mm of aluminium, so only gamma radiation is detected.
10	C	1	Use $A=\frac{N}{t}=\frac{30000}{5\times60}=100\,\text{Bq}$ (remember t must be converted into seconds)
11	A	1	Use $D=\frac{E}{m}=\frac{2\times10^{-3}}{0\cdot08}=0\cdot025\,\text{Gy}$
12	B	1	Use the Data sheet to obtain a value for the radiation weighting factor, w_r, for slow neutrons, which is 3, then use: $H=Dw_r=50\times10^{-3}\times3=0\cdot15$ Sv
13	E	1	You need to know the equivalent dose rate and exposure safety limits for the public and for workers in radiation industries in terms of annual effective equivalent dose required. Currently, the annual exposure safety limits are: 1 mSv for the public, 20 mSv for workers in radiation industries.
14	C	1	Hint – it is sometimes helpful to mark each quantity in the answers with 'v' for a vector and's' for a scalar to make the correct selection of the answer easier.
15	D	1	For average speed,use $d=vt$, $(50+30)=v\times8$, $v=10\,\text{ms}^{-1}$ For average velocity, use $s=\bar{v}t$, $(50-30)=\bar{v}\times8$, $\bar{v}=2\cdot5\,\text{ms}^{-1}$ South
16	A	1	Use acceleration $a=\frac{v-u}{t}=\frac{4-12}{8}=-1\text{ms}^{-2}$
17	E	1	Use $W=mg=1\times9\cdot8=9\cdot8\,N$ to calculate the weight of the ball. The weight of the ball is the downward force of gravity acting on the ball at all times.
18	C	1	Each ball takes the same time to reach sea level, because they are released from the same height and have the same vertical acceleration. Air resistance is ignored in this question, so there is no horizontal force acting on the balls; there is no horizontal acceleration. Different horizontal distances travelled mean that the horizontal velocities are different because the balls are in the air for the same time.

Question	Answer	Max mark	Hint
19	D	1	The horizontal section of the graph between 100 and 350 seconds indicates where the substance is changing state from solid to liquid. The energy supplied to the substance during this time is calculated using $P = \frac{E}{t}, 200 = \frac{E}{(350-100)}, E = 50\,000\,J$ To calculate specific latent heat of fusion of the substance use $E = ml_f, 50\,000 = 0.25 \times l_f, l_f = 2.0 \times 10^5\,JKg^{-1}$
20	E	1	Hint: use a ruler to find which element has all of its lines exactly matching the position of lines in the star spectrum.

SECTION 2

Question			Answer	Max mark	Hint
1	a)		$E_K = \frac{1}{2}mv^2$ (1) $= \frac{1}{2} \times 500 \times 55^2$ (1) $= 7{\cdot}6 \times 10^5$ J (1)	3	When using $E_K = \frac{1}{2}mv^2$ to calculate the kinetic energy, remember to multiply by the velocity squared.
	b)		$E_K \equiv E_p$ (1) $7{\cdot}6 \times 10^5 = mgh$ (1) $7{\cdot}6 \times 10^5 = 500 \times 9{\cdot}8 \times h$ (1) $h = 155$ m	3	Hint: When asked to show how a value is reached, take care to include important steps. First mark, awarded for a statement that energy is conserved i.e. that the kinetic energy of the water is transformed into potential energy. Second mark, awarded for stating the relationship used to calculate E_P. Third mark, awarded for showing how various quantities are used within the relationship $E_P = mgh$ which lead to the final answer.
	c)		Frictional forces between the jet and air cause some kinetic energy to be lost and not converted into potential energy.	1	As the water rises through the air, air friction causes some kinetic energy to be changed into heat and some sound energy, reducing the energy available to be converted into potential energy.
				(7)	
2	a)	(i)	2 V	1	Care is required when extracting data from graphs; a ruler is useful when obtaining these values.
		(ii)	Voltage across the capacitor is changing, so the voltage across the resistor is changing and so the current in the resistor changes.	1	Current is the rate of movement of charge in a conductor. As the capacitor charges, this rate reduces so the current reduces in its circuit.
		(iii)	$V_R = 3 - 2 = 1$V (1) $I = \frac{V}{R}$ (1) $= \frac{1}{2000}$ (1) $= 5 \times 10^{-4}$ A (1)	4	Use the voltage across the capacitor from a) (i) to calculate the voltage across the resistor after 3 minutes. Use Ohm's Law to determine the resistance of R.

Question			Answer	Max mark	Hint
	b)		The voltage across the capacitor increases (1) and reaches a value which will switch the MOSFET on (1) (to sound the buzzer)	2	The voltage across the capacitor increases and eventually has a value which will switch on MOSFET causing a current in the buzzer.
				(8)	
3	a)	(i)	$E_h = cm\Delta T$ (1) $= 4180 \times 250 \times 10{\cdot}3$ (1) $= 1{\cdot}1 \times 10^7$ J (1)	3	Temperature change, $\Delta T = (25{\cdot}8 - 15{\cdot}5) = 10{\cdot}3$ °C, must be calculated first. Then use $E_h = cm\,\Delta T$ to calculate the energy transferred into heat energy.
	b)		$P = \frac{E}{t}$ (1) $350 = \frac{1{\cdot}1 \times 10^7}{t}$ (1) $t = 3{\cdot}1 \times 10^4$ s $= 8{\cdot}6$ hours (1)	3	Use the value for heat energy calculated in a). The question requires the answer, in seconds, to be converted into hours: (t in hours $= \frac{3{\cdot}1 \times 10^4}{60 \times 60} = 8.6$ hours)
				(6)	
4	a)		20°C = 293 K $\frac{p_1 \times V_1}{T_1} = \frac{p_2 \times V_2}{T_2}$ (1) $\frac{1{\cdot}0 \times 10^5 \times 5{\cdot}0 \times 10^{-4}}{293}$ (1) $= \frac{5{\cdot}0 \times 10^6 \times 2{\cdot}0 \times 10^{-5}}{T_2}$ $T_2 = 586$ K (1)	3	The temperature before compression must be converted into kelvin before use in the relationship. It is not necessary to convert the final temperature back into °C unless the question specifically asks for this.
	b)	(i)	Pressure difference $= 7{\cdot}0 \times 10^6 - 1{\cdot}0 \times 10^5$ $= 6{\cdot}9 \times 10^6$ Pa (1) $P = \frac{F}{A}$ (1) $7{\cdot}0 \times 10^6 = \frac{F}{6{\cdot}4 \times 10^{-3}}$ (1) $F = 4{\cdot}48 \times 10^4$ N	3	First, calculate the pressure difference between inside and outside the cylinder. Then write $P = \frac{F}{A}$ Then substitute values into the relationship.
		(ii)	The volume of the air increases. There are fewer collisions between the air particles and the piston walls because the air particles must travel further between collisions. Fewer collisions means the force on the piston walls is reduced, so pressure reduces.	1	It is important to mention: volume increasing, fewer collisions so reduced force on cylinder walls, resulting in reduced pressure.
				(7)	

Question			Answer	Max mark	Hint
5	a)	(i)	$T = \frac{1}{f}$ (1) $= \frac{1}{0{\cdot}25}$ (1) $= 4\,\text{s}$ (1)	3	Remember that when the frequency is in Hz, the answer for T is in seconds.
		(ii)	$v = f\lambda$ $= 0{\cdot}25 \times 4$ $= 1\,\text{m}\,\text{s}^{-1}$	3	Remember to include the units for speed in the final answer.
		(iii)	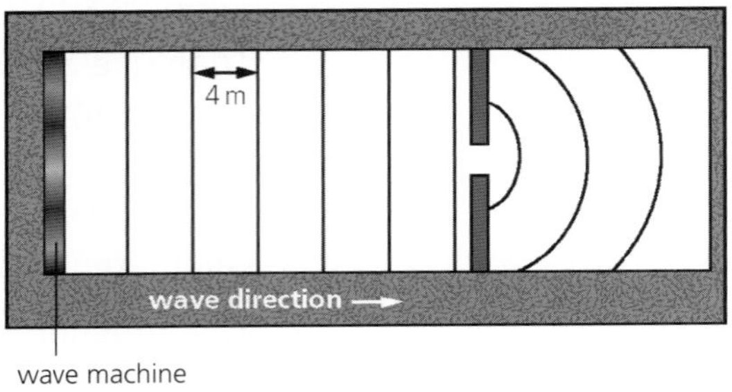	2	The diffracted waves after the barrier should: have the same wavelength as waves before the barrier (1) be circular and reach into the space beyond the barrier. (1)
	b)		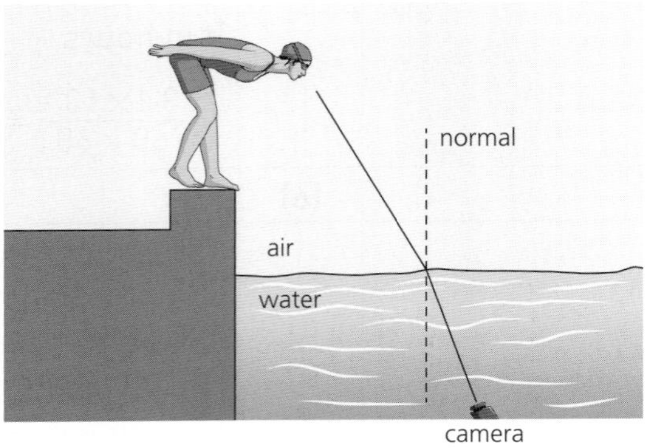	3	Marks for the drawing are awarded as follows: 1 mark for showing the light ray changing direction at the air/water boundary. 1 mark for the angle of refraction in water being less than the angle of refraction in air. 1 mark for the normal being correctly drawn at the point where the light ray meets the air/water boundary. It is good practice to use a ruler when drawing light rays.
				(11)	
6	a)	(i)	Infrared	1	The order of the bands of the electromagnetic spectrum should be memorised.
		(ii)	Photographic film	1	Other detectors of X-ray include: Geiger-Muller tube, Scintillation counter.
		(iii)	Radio waves have the lowest frequency.	1	The order of increasing energy transferred by the bands of the electromagnetic spectrum should be memorised.
		(iv)	Gamma radiation has the highest frequency.	1	The order of increasing frequency of these bands of the electromagnetic spectrum should be memorised.

Question			Answer	Max mark	Hint
	b)		$d = vt$ $2{\cdot}4 \times 10^{22} = 3 \times 10^{8} \times t$ $t = 8{\cdot}0 \times 10^{13}$s number of light years $= \frac{8.0 \times 10^{13}}{365.25 \times 24 \times 60 \times 60}$ $= 2{\cdot}5 \times 10^{6}$ light years	3	Use $d = vt$ to calculate the time, in seconds, for light to travel $2{\cdot}4 \times 10^{22}$ m, using $v = 3 \times 10^{8}$ m s^{-1}. Then calculate the no. of light years in this time. no.of light years $= \frac{\text{(total time in seconds)}}{\text{(number of seconds in one year)}}$ (number of seconds in one year $= 365 \times 24 \times 60 \times 60$)
	c)	(i)	Long wavelength signals diffract more around the Earth's curvature than short waves.	1	Wave diffraction is greater for longer wavelengths, so longer radio waves from a land based transmitter would diffract more around the curve of the Earth to reach ships which are far out on the sea.
		(ii)	$v = \frac{d}{t}$ (1) $3 \times 10^{8} = \frac{d}{0.0046}$ (1) $d = 1.38 \times 10^{6}$ m (1)	3	Radio waves travel at the speed of light.
				(11)	

Question			Answer	Max mark	Hint
7			**Sample answer** Nuclear radiation is used in treatment of cancer patients. For example, gamma rays are directed into the tumour site from different angles to destroy cancer cells, but to minimise the damage to healthy cells. X-rays are used to get images of the body. X-rays travel through the body and photographic film or image intensifiers produce images of bones, tissue etc. Ultrasound waves are used to obtain images inside the body. For example, to produce images of an unborn baby within the womb. An ultrasound transmitter sends signals into the mother's womb. The signals are reflected by the baby and received by a detector. A computer is used to process the data to provide an image, or moving images, of the baby. Infrared rays are used in the treatment of muscle injuries. Using ultrasound is less dangerous that using X-rays which can damage cells of the body. Radio waves are used in the treatment of certain cancerous tumours. A probe which produces high energy radio waves is directed into the tumour. The radio waves produce a current in the cells which heats them until they are destroyed.	3	This is an open-ended question: a variety of physics statements and descriptions can be used to answer this question. Marks are awarded on the basis of whether the answer overall demonstrates 'no', 'limited', 'reasonable' or 'good' understanding. Demonstrates no understanding 0 marks Demonstrates limited understanding: 1 mark Demonstrates reasonable understanding: 2 marks Demonstrates good understanding: 3 marks Three marks would be awarded to an answer which demonstrates a good understanding of the physics involved. The answer would show a good comprehension of the physics of the situation, provided in a logically correct sequence. (This type of answer might include a statement of the principles involved, a relationship or an equation, and the application of these to respond to the problem.) This does not mean the answer has to be what might be termed an 'excellent' answer or a 'complete' one. Also, note that the open-ended type of question is worth three marks. It is important not to spend too much time answering this question (3–4 minutes is the average time in the paper for 3 marks). A guide would be to take perhaps 3–5 minutes to complete this type of question. Only use more time than this if you have completed and checked all of the remaining questions in the paper.
				(3)	

Question			Answer	Max mark	Hint
8	a)		The lead box absorbs any background radiation.	1	Since background radiation is absorbed, the detected radiation is received only from the radioactive source.
	b)	(i)	Half-life is the time for the activity of a radio active substance to reduce to half of its original value.	1	The definition of half-life is a standard question and should be memorised.
		(ii)	Activity is 90 kBq at time 0; activity is 45 kBq at time 9 hours. The half-life is 9 hours.	1	It is convenient to start with 90 kBq which is at time zero, then find the time on the graph for half (45 kBq); this allows the time to be read directly (9 hours).
	c)	(i)	The radioisotope emits radiation. (1) Large container prevents carriers from close contact with radioisotope (1)	2	A safety precaution is to keep a distance between the radioisotope and the person carrying the box.
		(ii)	7am 5th–11 am 6th July = 28 hours 800 → 400 → 200 → 100 ≡ 3 half- lives ≡ 27 hours so below 100 kBq in 28 hours (1) So radioisotope should not be used. (1)	2	First, calculate the time interval between delivery and the proposed use of the radioisotope. After 3 half-lives (27 hours) the activity is 100 kBq, so after 28 hours, the activity would be below 100 kBq so the radioisotope should not be used.
				(7)	
9	a)	(i)	$a = \frac{v-u}{t}$ (1) $= \frac{80-0}{60}$ (1) $= 1{\cdot}3\,\text{ms}^{-1}$ (1)	3	Care is required to select the correct values for u (0 ms^{-1}) and v (80 ms^{-1}) from the graph, and to use them correctly in $a = \frac{v-u}{t}$.
		(ii)	unbalanced force $F_{un} = ma$ (1) $= 360\,000 \times 1{\cdot}3$ $= 468\,000$ N (1) average frictional force = forward force of engines $- F_{un}$ $= 500\,000 - 468\,000$ (1) average frictional force = 32 000N (1)	4	First calculate the unbalanced force required to produce the aircraft's acceleration using the value for acceleration calculated in a) (i). The forward force overcomes the average frictional force and provides the unbalanced accelerating force: forward force = average frictional force + F_{un}
		(iii)	Total distance = area under graph $= \frac{1}{2}bh$ (1) $= \frac{1}{2} \times 60 \times 80$ (1) $= 2400$ m (1)	3	The aircraft takes off after 60 seconds, so the total distance required during take-off is the area under the graph.

Question			Answer	Max mark	Hint
	b)		At constant height, upward force $=$ weight of aircraft $= mg$ (1) $= 360000 \times 9{\cdot}8$ (1) $= 3{\cdot}53 \times 10^6\,N$ (1)	3	When the aircraft's height is constant, the upward force on the aircraft and its weight are balanced.
	c)		Exposure time in 1 year $=$ time for one flight $\times$ number of flights $= 7 \times 106$ $= 742$ hours $\dot{H} = \frac{H}{t}$ (1) $8 \times 10^{-6} = \frac{H}{742}$ (1) $H = 5{\cdot}9\,mSv$ (1)	3	First, calculate the total number of hours of exposure. When writing the relationship, $\dot{H} = \frac{H}{t}$, it is important to correctly represent equivalent dose rate, $\dot{H}$, with a clearly marked dot above. Use time, t, in the same units as given in the question (hours).
				(16)	

Question			Answer	Max mark	Hint
10			**Sample answer** Newton 1: Stationary objects have balanced forces acting, e.g. when a person is sitting, their weight is balanced by an upward reaction force from the chair. Newton 2: When an unbalanced force acts on an object, it causes acceleration which is proportional to the size of the unbalanced force, e.g. when a vehicle accelerates from rest, an unbalanced force acts on it causing an acceleration which is proportional to the size of the unbalanced force acting on the vehicle and inversely proportional to the mass of the vehicle. Newton 3: There is an equal and opposite reaction force to every action force, e.g. when a person walks, their foot exerts a backward force on the ground, while the ground exerts a forward force on the foot, causing the person to move forward.	3	This is an open-ended question: a variety of physics statements and descriptions can be used to answer this question. Marks are awarded on the basis of whether the answer overall demonstrates 'no', 'limited', 'reasonable' or 'good' understanding. Demonstrates no understanding: 0 marks Demonstrates limited understanding: 1 mark Demonstrates reasonable understanding: 2 marks Demonstrates good understanding: 3 marks Three marks would be awarded to an answer which demonstrates a good understanding of the physics involved. The answer would show a good comprehension of the physics of the situation, provided in a logically correct sequence. (This type of answer might include a statement of the principles involved, a relationship or an equation, and the application of these to respond to the problem.) This does not mean the answer has to be what might be termed an 'excellent' answer or a 'complete' one. Also, note that the open-ended type of question is worth three marks. It is important not to spend too much time answering this question (3–4 minutes is the average time in the paper for 3 marks). A guide would be to take perhaps 3–5 minutes to complete this type of question. Only use more time than this if you have completed and checked all of the remaining questions in the paper.
				(3)	

Question			Answer	Max mark	Hint
11	**a)**	**(i)**	distance travelled = 125 – 11 = 114 km $E_W = Fd$ (1) $= 3{\cdot}7 \times 10^5 \times 114 \times 10^3$ (1) $= 4{\cdot}2 \times 10^{10}$ J (1)	3	Calculate the distance that the average frictional force acts across. Remember to convert km into m.
		(ii)	Friction between spacecraft and atmosphere produces heat energy which may cause damage to the contents of the spacecraft.	1	The contents (controls, apparatus etc.) of the spacecraft require protection from extreme temperatures.
		(iii)	Moon has no atmosphere so there would be no frictional forces acting on the parachute or spacecraft to slow it down.	1	Upward frictional forces acting on the parachute decelerated the spacecraft in the Martian atmosphere.
	b)	**(i)**	$W = mg$ (1) $12210 = m \times 3{\cdot}7$ (1) $m = 3300$ kg	2	Use the Data sheet to obtain the value for g, the gravitational field strength on Mars (3·7 N kg^{-1}).
		(ii)	upward unbalanced force = 18810 − 12210 = 6600 N (1) $F_{un} = ma$ (1) $6600 = 3300 \times a$ (1) $a = 2\ \text{m s}^{-2}$ (1)	4	First calculate the unbalanced upward decelerating force. Since the question asks for the magnitude of the deceleration, it is not necessary to include a negative sign.
				(11)